A LIFE IN EDUCATION

A LIFE IN EDUCATION

Brian Simon

Lawrence & Wishart
LONDON

Lawrence & Wishart Limited
99a Wallis Road
London E9 5LN

First published 1998

British Library Cataloguing in Publication data.
A catalogue record for this book is available from the
British Library.

ISBN 0 85315 8665

Photoset in North Wales by
Derek Doyle & Associates, Mold, Flintshire.
Printed and bound in Great Britain by
Redwood Books Ltd, Trowbridge.

CONTENTS

Dedicated to the memory of
Sam Fisher, Robin Pedley,
Harry Rée, Edward Blishen,
Raymond King, Brian Jackson,
Margaret Miles,
and all co-fighters for
comprehensive secondary
education who have passed away

INTRODUCTION

I have been fortunate to work in the field of education throughout my life – one of the most worthwhile in which to be engaged, alongside numerous dedicated and enthusiastic colleagues. Never can a profession – teaching – have been subjected to so much ignorant criticism, if not coarse abuse, by the Conservative administrations of the 1980s and 1990s. Men and women qualified in a variety of specialisms and with a wealth of experience have been subjected to orders from what might be termed 'managerial level' operating to narrow the scope of education, confining it within a bureaucratically defined strait-jacket. Over the past eighteen years a deliberate attempt has been made to ensure decision-making is determined by the crude operation of market forces. The damage done has been immense. But finally, on 1st May 1997, the various countries of Great Britain defeated decisively the Conservative government's attempt to win yet another term; threatening yet further fracturing measures. The 'New Labour' administration have hit the ground running. Early measures gave a new hope for the future; there will now be an attempt genuinely to involve all in planning the future – teachers, parents, governors, local authorities, industry, as well as government. There is a great deal that needs doing. But, as the twentieth century draws to a close we may, at last, look forward hopefully to the new millennium.

1996 marked the fiftieth anniversary of my own entry into teaching – in what was then categorised as an all-age, and so still 'elementary' school. This experience provides a certain perspective on contemporary problems now hotly disputed. For instance the latest advice on what should be done to raise standards in the schools of the 1990s, said to derive from East Asia, was in fact the standard pattern in operation when I began teaching in English schools. The degree of confusion engendered over the past eighteen years seems due directly to the politicisation of education, now more evident than ever was the case in the past; and this at a time when not only parents but many others with responsibilities, for instance school governors, need to understand the issues at stake – the steps that can aid the children and schools in their care and enable them to do a sound and effective job with such resources as governments are prepared to make available.

Having been engaged for several decades at different levels of the school system, I have something to say about all this. For one thing it is essential to recognise for what they are, contemporary arguments about testing, league tables, and co-operative teaching methods. I have witnessed the introduction and manoeuvring of such measures down the years – the use of intelligence testing to legitimise selection yesterday and promise of 'variety' today is a good example. It is important that this 'pattern of development' should be understood by the present generation.

I did not enter full-time teaching until I reached thirty years of age. Born in 1915, when the first major war of the century was well underway – three uncles killed, two with young families which my father had then to look after – I finished university shortly before the Second World War started. Both parents came from the middle class – sufficiently affluent – both from extended families which sent children to 'preparatory' and 'public' schools and, if male, to Oxford and Cambridge, duly paying all fees and costs. But in my case there were advantages in having two education-oriented parents, both also closely concerned with civic affairs. My father, Ernest Darwin Simon, educated as an engineer and chairman of the two family firms established by *his* father, deliberately devolved responsibilities and gave over half his time to public affairs (in the 1930s to a well-organised campaign for the introduction of Education for Citizenship, seen as an answer to dictatorial regimes now in the ascendant, particularly Nazism). Later he was a fully involved chairman of a University Council (Manchester). Ernest Simon moved from Liberalism (being a Member of Parliament twice in the inter-war years) to Labour – being appointed Chairman of the Board of Governors of the BBC by Attlee in 1947, having accepted a peerage from the same source earlier that year.

My mother, Shena D. Simon, joined the Labour Party in 1935 as a direct reaction to Tory educational policy of that year. She remained an active member of the Manchester Education Committee, of which she had been Chair in the early 1930s, for over forty years. A member of the Consultative Committee to the Board of Education, she was one of the signatories of the 'Spens' Report published late in 1938 (on the future of secondary education), later publishing the first popular book propagating the comprehensive secondary school *Three Schools or One?* Shena Simon had a profound and detailed knowledge of educational administration, becoming probably the leading expert in the country. In her educational work she formed a close partnership with R.H. Tawney, whose place she had taken on the Consultative Committee, and who remained a very close friend of both my parents all their lives.

Looking back I can recognise both parents as consistently supportive of all I achieved in education. My father never pressed me to take up engineering and join what was still very much a family firm, if greatly expanded since my grandfather's days, though several members of our extended family did so. Both parents believed that a career in public service (and perhaps politics) was the more desirable aim. Both tended to see educational administration as a suitable career for me as my own interest in education generally ripened – and for my brother a career in local government. But both sons were inevitably subjected to the crisis situation of the 1930s and, during my time at university I began to take my own road.

Much has been written on 1930s Cambridge and the concomitant movement of a generation of students to embracing a Communist outlook. The swing to the left which involved many at Oxbridge and elsewhere at this time did not take place because students were interested in politics in the abstract, wrote the then leading young student, John Cornford. (Cornford was an exact contemporary of mine at university (and college) and was one of the first to join the International Brigade in Spain, being tragically killed on the Cordoba front on the eve of his 21st birthday in December 1936 – a death which had a profound and lasting impact on many of his contemporaries.[1]) Students shifted to the left 'because the actual conditions of their lives', the actual problems confronting them, 'forced them steadily though hesitatingly to a revolutionary position', to a recognition of the need for fundamental change. There was no need to be interested in politics to recognise the 'ever-widening gap between the potentialities of science, technique, culture, and education' and the actual realisation of these in contemporary society. They saw food destroyed when people went hungry; children suffering from rickets failing reparable action. Yet their higher education evaded rather than tackled such problems and their possible solution. In the meantime, the history student of 1936 was still being taught a 'theory of the modern state' deriving from the day before yesterday. 'The course nowhere says what a Soviet is, nowhere makes room for an analysis of Fascism, is completely incapable of dealing with any modern political development'. That is why interest in political and social developments led to Marxism 'which gives the tools for such analysis', and so to support for the Communist Party. For many of my generation, this was a formative influence, strengthened as the many problems of capitalism remained unsolved, evils continued unchecked, fascism extended its power – leading to a second world war barely a quarter of a century after the close of the first.

For me, this movement of opinion and action had a lasting influence. I have written on various aspects of this involvement since – socialist aims, Marxist outlook, Communist party politics, in which I was involved. I ceased direct political activity in this sense in the early 1970s, and retired from the university at age 65 in 1980.

But in this book the focus is directly on *educational* issues and how these have been treated down the years. This is no autobiography detailing personal feelings, family affairs, friends. Drawing on contemporary experience at different stages it attempts to unravel how opinions were formed, what kind of investigation and research was undertaken at different levels and why. All these matters, and many others, were closely relevant to the education of students – their preparation as teachers – my task when I moved to university work in 1950. This involved a focus on the study of the process of education itself, on the nature of learning and teaching, on classroom organisation and its variations – culminating, perhaps, in my case, in the ORACLE research project into primary education in which I was deeply involved for a full decade (1970-1980). It also involved systematic and detailed historical study of educational developments over the last two centuries in an effort to under-stand and explicate how we had arrived where we are – also close study of the local history of schooling, of its community aspects leading to intensive involvement in the whole development of comprehensive secondary education. The study of teaching and learning led into the whole confusing field of educational psychology; into the rigorous examination, and critique, of intelligence testing and the claims made for this 'science', and so into interest in the work and outlook of the outstanding Russian psychologist A.R. Luria and his brilliant mentor Lev Vygotski. These interests led also to the field of educational journalism with the launch, in 1958, of the educational journal Forum, now in its 40th year.

Through all this I have been exceptionally fortunate in being able to work in partnership with Joan Simon, who has shared, and contributed, to all these interests and spheres of activity. Married at one of the blackest moments in the last war (1941), we were able to settle down together from late 1945 and have co-operated in various aspects of the work including study of Leicestershire's historical development from the sixteenth century. When our interest in Russian psychology peaked in the early 1960s, Joan translated many articles for the publication that emerged, as well as a striking book by Luria which opened up in a new way the whole crucial issue of the role of language in mental development. She also contributed to the journal Forum from 1958, particularly a set of articles monitoring the early swing to comprehensive education. In the mid-1960s Joan published a thorough scholarly study based on intensive research which transformed the whole interpretation of 16th century educational developments. This co-operation continues as we both march on into our eighties.

Developments over the last sixty years are treated chronologically in this book, as an investigation as to how different aspects of these activities came about, their motivation, and how each relates to the other. To attempt such an analysis – as it were, to make sense of a lifetime's activity – is of interest to me. In the welter of events it is not always easy to see one's way; looking back, a pattern guiding development begins to emerge. But I hope also that this book, or record, will be informative in outcome, and throw light on what has been inherited, adapted and added to over the last half century.

NOTES

1. Pat Sloan, ed., 'Notes on the Teaching of History at Cambridge', pp. 151-58, and 'Communism in the Universities', in *John Cornford, A Memoir*, London 1938, pp159-69.

1
BEGINNINGS

I date my first, and as it proved decisive, involvement in education to a chance happening. Quite early in my first year as a student at Cambridge, a friend – a girl from the co-educational and then innovative school, Bedales – called at my remote lodgings in Jesus Lane to take me, almost by force, to a nearby meeting in a small hall. It was organised by the Cambridge University Education Society which consisted mainly of undergraduates from 'public schools' interested in new kinds of schools. This small society was not connected in any way to the university education department where post-graduates followed a one year 'Diploma' course to qualify as 'recognised' teachers. These students were known as 'Fox's Martyrs', after the then head, Charles Fox, while the department itself had never made any serious impact either on university life or on educational policy and practice at large. Most Education Society members had an interest in schooling without necessarily thinking of becoming teachers. A few senior members of the university supported the society, notably Joan Bennett from the English faculty; a more idiosyncratic member being Mrs Broad, the well-known wife of the Professor of Moral Sciences, who delighted us by smoking a short stubbly pipe throughout our meetings. There was also helpful support from Ernest Barker, then Professor of Politics or political science.

Most of us knew nothing of the state or 'maintained' system of education, or of its schools, having been educated outside it. But my case was somewhat different in that both my parents were greatly interested in educational matters in one way or another, as well as in civic affairs. In the mid-1930s, when I was at university, my father launched the Association for Education in Citizenship, to which he devoted an immense amount of time and energy. During this time my mother worked whole-heartedly as an active member of the Manchester Education Committee and of the Consultative Committee. So naturally I became familiar, if at second hand, with some of the problems of the state or 'maintained' system of education.

However my own education was experienced in the 'independent' sector. I had been sent, with an elder brother, to a recently established, modernised 'public school', Gresham's, at Holt in Norfolk – a school which at the time appealed to the more radical middle class. Here the forceful head, J.R. Eccles, a passionate supporter of the Liberal party, set out to create a humanist environment with no school *rules*, only 'traditions'; corporal punishment was excluded, friendly relationships between teachers and pupils were encouraged, as also between older and younger boys. To this end the school depended on the 'honour system', later much criticised by Wystan Auden, a pupil before my day. My time at Gresham's certainly fuelled my interest in education; an interest enhanced by two terms at a remarkable German school, run by Kurt Hahn in Salem, in Southern Germany.

Salem in 1933 was far removed from my experience of English public schooling; it was both fascinating and dramatic. Hahn ran the school as a sort of boys' (and girls') republic under his aegis; other teachers counted for little. His main concern was to find the potential (artistic, intellectual, physical) which he believed existed in *every* pupil, and also the means by which this could be given full rein and encouragement. He was also deeply concerned with moral issues, haranguing the whole school if he felt it necessary.

But in March 1933, two or three days after the election of the Nazi party, Salem was surrounded with Brown Shirts (SA men) and Hahn brutally hauled off to jail at Überlingen, three miles away on the shores of the Bodensee. He had very courageously, and on several occasions, spoken out quite overtly challenging the Nazi leadership and policies, and was well known nationally for his courage and resistance. He was, in fact, one of the very first of Hitler's opponents to be persecuted. Pressure from England (where he had friends in high places), ensured Hahn's release but he was banned from returning to Salem. As is well known, he escaped to England some months later, finally establishing his new school (boys only) at Gordonstoun in Scotland.

I remained at Salem through the summer and thus gained an insight into Hahn's educational purposes and procedures. This certainly stimulated my thinking about education, particularly his stress on human potentiality as well as his imaginative approach to its release, which depended on a close knowledge of the individual. I only saw Hahn in his role as Head for a short time between January and March 1933 – and even then he frequently journeyed to Berlin, advising Brüning and other centre politicians. But his style as Head, his close attention to individual pupils, his own teaching (of Shakespeare), and the excitement of knowing that anything might happen any day (a Hahn edict: the whole school will immediately go skiing) have remained with me. I visited Hahn twice later in the 1930s at Gordonstoun and retained that admiration for his character, style and determination, though not sharing his concern for an aristocratic education.

This had been a special experience. For the most part we in the 'Cambridge University Education Society' were interested in the more 'progressive' wing of the 'public schools' sector, in the pioneer co-educational Bedales, for instance (where I spent a fortnight one summer, supervising the School Certificate examination), and Abbotsholme, a school that had aroused Kurt Hahn's enthusiasm well before World War One. In particular we sought to find out about the more way-out progressive schools for the middle and professional classes which burgeoned in the 1920s and 1930s. Among the speakers invited for our weekly meetings were W.B. Curry of Dartington, then making a name as a leading independent progressive school; Dora Russell who, with her husband Bertrand, had founded Beacon Hill; the heads of the Burgess Hill School; Forest Hill School, and, perhaps most memorably, A.S. Neill of Summerhill. Some of our speakers had an international reputation and drew large audiences. Alfred Adler, then a guru of the psycho-analytic world but having differences with both Freud and Jung, drew in the crowds, but the largest meeting we sponsored was for Maria Montessori. At the height of her influence in the 1930s she visited Cambridge as part of a tour of the country, amidst a court of supporters; among these her son and general staff manager Mario, and for some reason the novelist Phyllis Bottome. Tea at the University Arms Hotel, a stately occasion, preceded the meeting, when the largest lecture theatre in the Mill Lane lecture rooms was packed to the brim. Presided over by Ernest Barker – a very effective, avuncular and friendly chairman – this was a memorable occasion.

UNIVERSITY ENQUIRY

I joined the Communist Party early in 1935, recruited by contemporaries at Trinity College, a focal point of student politics headed by a Gresham's acquaintance James Klugmann and John Cornford. During my final year, 1936-1937, political and educational interests fused in the promotion of a critical student enquiry into the content of education and teaching methods of the university. Although we were unaware of this, a similar concern was surfacing among students more generally, at Oxford, London University and in the civic (or 'modern') universities generally. These moves were in due course co-ordinated by the National Union of Students, a matter to be returned to. But Cambridge at the time had no Students Representative Council; the Union being largely a debating society and club, recruiting members by voluntary subscription. Attempts were made to unite the Cambridge union with NUS, but any arrangement was temporary and soon collapsed. In short Cambridge had no single body fully representing all students, on a par with the great student unions at all civic universities. Not only had we no functional contact with the NUS, there was no knowledge of or interest in it.

The establishment of Marxist study groups and the like in the mid-1930s tapped into the dissatisfaction of students with the educational content and procedures at Cambridge. Between 1936 and 1939 there was a growing determination among Cambridge students to reform and transform both curricula and teaching methods, and to claim some degree of functional involvement in arcane decision-making processes, from which students were then totally excluded. Historians were among those taking the lead in this movement, men such as Sam Fisher – later to become a respected teacher – attributed student intolerance to 'the bankruptcy and aridity of much that was taught', a shortcoming compounded by the poor quality of lectures. John Cornford's 'Notes on the Teaching of History at Cambridge' belongs to this period, and is a sharp condemnation of almost every aspect of the Cambridge approach – the confusion of aims, overt reliance on Hegelian idealism, the tightly bound particularity of the subject, in conjunction with insularity and provincialism. Similar, if less sharp and pointed, criticisms were expressed in Faculty Society meetings across the board – in the English Club, the Modern Language Society, the Moral Sciences Society, among mathematicians, scientists, economists, engineers, and medical students.

In my final year I was acting as president of the Education Society. I believed that this group could best ensure that criticisms were coherently formulated and brought to the attention of the authorities – that is the faculty boards. A subsidiary objective was to move towards an inter-faculty coordinating committee to represent student opinion generally, and which could negotiate with the university authorities on the model of the student unions in the civic universities. The efforts of the Education Society did have some effect; in the autumn of 1936 the society ran a well attended meeting chaired by Ernest Barker entitled 'Education in this University', which engaged in a broad discussion on lectures, examinations and seminars. There followed an invitation, to the secretaries of all faculty societies, to a meeting in my relatively capacious rooms in Trinity Street. All the leading societies sent representatives.

The next academic year saw a series of concentrated enquiries by each faculty society, often involving questionnaires to all students, draft reports being discussed and amended at society meetings, leading up to a final report presented to each faculty board. The representatives of the history faculty at the Education Society's meetings in 1936-37 went on to become well known historians and worked in university positions, one as President of a Cambridge college, another as Vice Chancellor of Oxford University. Four of the students who signed the detailed and highly critical report on the English Faculty later made important contributions to English studies: Boris Ford, Charles Barber, Leo Salinger, Frank Whitehead. The Economics (Marshall) Society report, again a lengthy but perhaps too detailed critique, was masterminded by Christopher Simon (a cousin) among others. 'Ah! the student Soviet!', said Joan Robinson, leading member of the faculty, welcoming us as she opened her door to let us in, bearing the draft report for discussion.

Two letters to the *Cambridge Review*, read by authority, reported on these activities. 'Some dons are beginning to get worried about [these] activities', runs a letter to my father enclosing copies, 'while others welcome them'. Some were 'frightened that the reports will contain criticism of them or their lectures. A little healthy fear will do them no harm, but I hope the authorities won't sit on it'. 'I have read your two letters to the *Cambridge Review* again', my father replied, 'and congratulate you on your initiative and on the way you are tackling this job'. But if the first was 'really excellent' the second was not so good – 'the meaning has to be rather energetically hunted for in places' (I found his copy with several pencilled corrections decades later).

Some dons were sympathetic – in particular Joan Robinson, and also Ernest Barker, who to some extent took us under his wing and also assured me he thoroughly approved our initiative. This critique of university procedures was a formative experience. It involved us in the study of very real issues ensuring that education ceased to remain a theoretical or remote issue, as its serious application to everyday life and relation to political affairs emerged. Subsequent experience, deriving immediately from this Cambridge movement, was to lock me into education, recognised as an increasingly urgent, relevant and congenial area of activity.

In the circumstances it was not difficult to decide to work in education, and, in order to do so to take a year's training as a teacher. There was no need for this had I been intending to teach in preparatory or 'public' schools – a university degree sufficed for that. But it was my intention to qualify professionally to teach in the nation's schools, and for this a course leading to a professional qualification was necessary.

The decision had parental approval although I had already spent four years at Cambridge due to a switch from the English tripos (after Part I, which took two years) to Part II of the Economics tripos (also two years) – an unusual combination but one which proved useful later. But there was no question of spending another year there when there was a much better place to study – what had once been the London Day Training College but in 1932 became the Institute of Education of London University. This was certainly at that time, as now, the leading national centre for educational studies with the redoubtable Sir Percy Nunn as Principal (shortly to be replaced by a true innovator, Fred Clarke).

I had already had good reports of the Institute from Harry Rée, a friend from Cambridge and indeed from my Manchester childhood, who had already got thoroughly hooked on education partly through his friendship with Henry Morris, Cambridgeshire's innovative chief education officer and inventor of village colleges. He had just completed his year when I entered and was now teaching at a grammar school. I was not to be disappointed.

Offered a place after being interviewed, I could take a holiday with a free mind; and had an idyllic one with friends sailing down the Dalmatian coast. So, in the autumn of 1937, I was ready for a new start, in new surroundings.

2

EMERGENCE

PREPARING FOR TEACHING

Teacher training has never had a good press; while university education departments, with some exceptions, have seldom been highly regarded. In the 1930s, and indeed much later, graduation itself carried with it qualified teacher status. The one year 'diploma' course offered by universities from the 1890s was not a necessary requirement for teaching in secondary schools – indeed was considered actually undesirable by 'public' schools. But, while many graduates went straight into teaching, a fully professional career in the world of education required extensive post-graduate study. Further, the course both provided an induction into teaching itself and allowed for study and discussion of the broader issues concerning education as a social phenomenon – its aims, procedures and organisation, including psychological, historical and sociological analysis. This was as much the case in the 1930s as it was until the 1980s. Today, with the emphasis on management, and competition in the form of league tables, this whole approach is less common. I count myself fortunate to have experienced it.

The Institute of Education emerged during the inter-war period to become the leading university-based centre in the Commonwealth for the study of education and the training of teachers. Closely linked historically to the London County Council – Sidney Webb had had a hand in its foundation early in the century – its main function was to provide a professional training for graduates preparing to teach, in both the elementary and secondary systems (the two then ran parallel). But it also provided advanced courses for practising teachers including groups from the Dominions (Canada, Australia, South Africa), and was involved in research and the supervision of higher degrees in education. These were relatively new functions sixty years ago, but the stimulus influenced the Institute and, with the appointment of Fred Clarke as Director in 1936, just before I entered, this seemed a forward-looking, innovative organisation at odds with the stagnation imposed on the nation's schools in the bleak inter-war years. Things were beginning to move.

I have titled this chapter 'Emergence' because, so far as my personal life was concerned, new opportunities presented themselves. The year at the Institute brought active involvement in teaching young people. These activities became my world, embraced with enthusiasm, providing a clear direction. But during the year, other, related, spheres opened up. Close involvement with the National Union of Students – I was elected as vice-president at the close of the academic year in July 1938 – came about partly by chance but was to prove formative. Also, perhaps unusually, appointment to the Labour Party's newly established Education Advisory Committee brought an early acquaintance with policy making on a national level. These experiences helped determine my own direction for the future, as will become clear.

The Institute's base was a large, five-storey, utilitarian building in Southampton Row, originally erected as a School of Architecture. It was a far cry from the Great Court at Trinity but was a friendly place, full of bustling activity, with staff and students merging most effectively. In the event of civil commotion, we used to feel, it would be good to hold the Institute since, set at a slight angle near the High Holborn Road crossing, it commanded the whole of Southampton Row to Aldwych to the south, and up to Euston Road north. The Spanish syndrome was much in our minds in those days!

The staff at the Institute – at least those that we, as 'Diploma' students, came across – were an interesting and lively group, a small one, of course, by comparison with the massive numbers there today, after nearly sixty years of continuous growth. The choice of Fred Clarke as director marked a transition from the biological approach favoured by his predecessor Percy Nunn – from psychometric and individualistic to a sociologically oriented, critical, more open and questioning form of analysis. As Clarke had spent the greater proportion of his life in South Africa and Canada, he approached English educational problems with a fresh eye, much less ready than most of his contemporaries to take current prejudices and modes of thought for granted. It was Clarke who was to persuade the noted Hungarian sociologist Karl Mannheim to join the staff, part-time, in 1940. Shortly after this Clarke's *Education and Social Change* appeared, concise and packed with new ideas about the study of education. It had a profound influence, not least on my own work. Unfortunately, Clarke was unwell during most of my year – he lectured, seated I remember, only twice; nevertheless the impression he made remains. In the post-war years he figured as the leading educational statesman in Britain, the first chairman of the Central Advisory Council for Education (England), established under the 1944 Education Act to further educational advance.

Among staff members who made an impact on the students were M.V.C. Jeffreys, Joseph Lauwerys (a leading comparativist), and especially the ardent German expatriate Reinhold Schairer, recruited at the start of my year at the Institute. Jeffreys, responsible for those preparing to teach history, was creatively involved in defining appropriate pedagogical means, a matter provoking much discussion at that time. But he also had philosophical and theological interests, being a kind of Christian Marxist of the Reinhold Niebuhr variety with a profoundly serious approach; he later became a professor at Birmingham University.

Lauwerys, of Belgian origin, was a sparkling character. Although relatively young, he had acquired an international reputation as student and exponent of comparative education, and he also kept abreast of scientific developments focusing especially on their social and educational implications. A brilliant lecturer, he came across as a sympathetic and highly intelligent person who shared his interests and enthusiasms very effectively with the students. As such he had been a welcome speaker to the Cambridge University Education Society. With Lauwerys you felt in touch with modern developments across the board.

Reinhold Schairer had been forced to leave his manifold activities among German youth and students on Hitler's accession to power. He was an enthusiastic, indeed impassioned, liberal educationist, profoundly anti-fascist, who became a friend and ally in the work of the National Union of Students. During my year at the Institute, as head of the new department of international studies, he took a group of advanced 'colonial' students on a fortnight's visit to schools and colleges in Paris and Brussels – a memorable experience. Above all, during the year, he delivered a course of 'inspirational' lectures on 'Great Educators' – an update of the traditional approach and one he invested with enormous enthusiasm. Included, of course, were Rousseau, Pestalozzi, Froebel – the 'progressive' tradition generally – finishing up, as I well remember, with the Italian (fascist) educator Gentile, who espoused and developed specific aspects of the progressive tradition. Gentile was appointed minister of education following Mussolini's seizure of power. His outlook, or philosophy of education, was to be sharply criticised, in due course, by Antonio Gramsci. But for Schairer, paradoxically, Gentile was something of a hero.

But there were others too, for instance my own tutor Dr P. Gurrey, responsible for English students. Gentle, intelligent, consistently encouraging, he did not set out to make an impact nor adhere to a particular school of thought; he just did the job quietly and well. He was, I think, overworked – in any case during the entire year he came to see me teach only twice. There was no 'method' teaching of the intensive kind later developed at Leicester University. Our tutor did, however, use lectures to induct us into relevant approaches and when he did visit gave good advice. N.V. Scarfe, the geographer, young, handsome, very energetic, made a big impression first at the Institute, then abroad. As professor and head of the education department at the University of British Columbia, he developed a wide network of related institutions throughout Western Canada, known to the educational world as 'Scarfeland'. As a Visiting Professor at UBC a few years ago, I had the pleasure of meeting him once again, now well into his eighties, but alert and vigorous.

In the 1930s psychology, history, philosophy, and other core subjects, such as health education, were taught – usually – by mass lectures delivered consecutively on Friday mornings in the newly built Senate House of the university in Russell Square. These were attended by hundreds of students from related institutions in the London area. Professor Hamley, who had taken over when Cyril Burt moved to a Chair at University College, lectured on psychology. The history of education was covered by A.C.F. Beales (from King's College, London), an outstanding lecturer who won our hearts by bringing his exposition right up to date, even including the NUS. Finally, to my surprise, also a lecturer was Geoffrey Winthrop Young, a distinguished mountaineer who, as a friend of Hahn's and Salem, had invited me to one of his annual climbing parties at Pen-Y-Pass near Snowden in 1933. He was indeed 'Reader' in comparative education at King's College, and had earlier been one of His Majesty's Inspectors of Schools. It did not seem to us that his heart was in it, as it certainly was in mountaineering. Finally Charles Lofthouse, well known in London's musical world, should be remembered. A fairly rotund, extrovert character, he taught us to sing and to function as a choir. Having been recruited to the Salem choir, I participated and found it highly enjoyable. Lofthouse certainly humanised what might have been a bleak and somewhat philistine environment and enhanced the value of the whole enterprise.

Enough has been said to suggest that I found the Institute interesting, even exciting, as a way towards a job in 'the real world'. I was among a group of very lively students of whom Charles Barber, of the English Faculty Survey, was one. He delivered a brilliant 'demonstration' lesson early in our year, which, in my view, deserved a medal. It was on a Wilfred Owen poem, to an elementary school class brought in for the purpose, a type of exercise long since abandoned. Generally speaking, my fellow students were interested in education, if critical – here, again, we produced an analysis and critique of our course, part of the Zeitgeist of the time. Relatively small, informal in its procedures, crammed into an old-fashioned and rickety building, the London Institute provided a first class environment for entry into education.

The study of education as a discipline was, of course, at an early stage. Few studies of a high quality were to hand; the amount of research carried out minimal. All this was to change, but not for thirty years or so, towards the late 1960s. Three books formed our bibles: Cyril Burt's *The Backward Child* (just published in 1936); an historical assessment, by G.A.N. Lowndes, *The Silent Revolution* (published in 1937), useful but bland; and, something of a classic, Percy Nunn's *Education, its Data and First Principles* (1920), which by its title appeared to pre-empt truth right across the board. By 1945 this famous text had been through some twenty printings and two revisions. Highly technical for the non-biologist, focusing almost totally on individual development, this provided no view of education as a social function, but epitomised yesterday's thinking. By the late 1930s this book, insofar as it could be understood, seemed to offer a dusty answer to most of our questions. Also available, of course, were Susan Isaacs's two classics, *Intellectual Growth in Young Children* (1930) and *Social Development in Young Children* (1933) which drew widely on actual experience at the experimental Malting House School in Cambridge, which our Education Society had visited. But if these offered a more realistic analysis than Percy Nunn, their relevance to the needs of children in over-crowded elementary schools up and down the country was hard to discern. Malting House was a private school catering mainly for the offspring of Cambridge dons.

Teaching though was at the heart of the year's experience and the crucial factor in determining success. How effective could one be in the classroom? How far would it be possible to engage the interest and involvement of thirty or more children? What could be achieved? Facing a class of children for the first time can be a fairly traumatic experience, certainly in the early months of the training year.

The system was to attach groups of three or four students to a long-suffering school in London for a fortnight before the university year began. Up beyond Kings Cross, in Islington, there was a very traditional, but well-run elementary school, for boys between 11 and 14, of the kind then known as a 'senior' school (resulting from the 'Hadow reorganisation' proposals of 1926). Here we took our first lessons. Tutorial help was minimal, no-one visited us during the preliminary fortnight. Later, after term started, individuals were attached to a specific school, teaching there regularly two days a week throughout the year. My tutor (Gurrey) visited me twice during the rest of the year, as already mentioned. His proper job was lecturing on teaching, so it may have been that staffing problems precluded fuller involvement. Thirteen years later, as a tutor at Leicester, under the system set up by Professor Tibble, I accompanied students on a similar preliminary fortnight, students who taught them-selves and observed others (including their lecturer). I continued to visit these students roughly once a week during the year, but in those pre-war days much was left to the students themselves.

'I have just finished my first lesson', runs one of a series of letters to a friend, apparently immediately it was over. I had prepared for forty minutes and was surprised to have been allo-cated a full hour. I had taken the class through the ballad of Sir Patrick Spens 'which they loved and that pleased me a lot'. The class teacher, sitting in on the class, then went out and I took them through another ballad, getting them to join in the refrain. 'They liked that too'. Discipline was not too bad though towards the end some had got a bit restive, 'an hour was too long'. The class then asked to read 'The Charge of the Light Brigade', so 'I let them and they read it with great gusto'. The lesson, I wrote, 'was fun, but jolly hard work!'. That was my first lesson survived. The following week we each took, and so prepared, two or three lessons a day.

For my main teaching practice throughout the rest of the year

I was allocated to the City of London School. A 'direct grant' boys grammar, serving London's professional class, this was classified as a 'public school' since its head was a member of the Head Masters' Conference (HMC). Mainly I taught English, but, since I had two strings to my bow, I was also given the opportunity of teaching social studies to sixth-form pupils. Preparing lessons of this kind was a responsibility of mine throughout the year.

Sixth-form teaching presented no serious problems from the pedagogic point of view but, for the novice teacher, lacking tuition, the younger classes certainly did. Although, of course, all these children were specially selected (or their parents could afford the fees), they were a lively lot and were at times difficult to control, during my first term at least. Clearly, from my letters at the time, I was much too easy with my younger classes at the start and soon realised that friendly relations were not enough, and that I should have shown a firm and unyielding exterior. A lesson which my tutor attended got almost completely out of hand, but his advice resulted in tactics to quell rebellion, in this and other classes. A letter reported: 'I have quelled both my two forms now; the one this morning, which I thought was going to be very difficult indeed, was really quiet all the way through. I strode in, was fearfully stern for three minutes, and then they shut up. Thank God!' Was it really as easy as that, I wonder now?

If I focus on the disciplinary side it is because to master this was essential for survival. Success clearly requires both effective means of control and finding the way to interest and involve pupils in the work in hand – in other words painstaking preparation and clear objectives. My tutor's second visit several months later in March 1938 provided an occasion to drive this home after watching me teach morning and afternoon. 'He criticised me hard and strong for some forty minutes', I reported, but was 'quite pleased with one of the lessons he saw and gave a lot of valuable advice'. Gurrey had stressed that I should think more about the aim of each individual lesson, and 'that is what I am going to do till midnight'. So at least, it seems, he had driven his point home.

Sixth-form teaching presented entirely different problems – and opportunities. The class was taken by a very lively, friendly and helpful teacher called Wilmot,who gave me a very free hand and full support (his brother was later appointed Minister of Supply in Attlee's 1945 administration). With a class of about twelve the work, on nineteenth century social and economic trends, could be individualised as specific research projects. Each boy was allotted a topic, all producing graphic representations based on relevant data. 'They pore over books full of statistics', I wrote, 'trying to get the relevant ones and they get them too. And they cull them from friends and libraries out of school'. This was the Economics Sixth, a joy to teach, ready to follow up projects in their spare time, and letting out great sighs when our forty minutes ended.

If this was feather-bedded teaching, it was valuable experience. In the summer I evidently took a leaf out of *Culture and Environment* (1932), a book by F.R. Leavis, co-authored by Denys Thompson, my youthful and very stimulating English teacher at Gresham's. For all the members of my sixth-form came with a daily newspaper of their choice and settled down to make a precise analysis of its contents, drawing diagrams and writing essays. One might say that this was a precursor to the post-war world of education.

The Institute course closed at the end of the summer term with an examination covering both teaching and theory. Of course we had notice of the lesson to be assessed by both an internal and an external examiner. I spent two and a half hours preparing this lesson, 'it ought to be pretty slick'; it was apparently 'quite successful' – the boys had in the event, supported me and having them on one's side on these occasions was at least half the battle! I was, however, totally alienated by the written examination which I couldn't take seriously – spending the morning reading a novel and then scribbling '*the* most utter nonsense for three hours without stopping'. Some of the questions, I felt, did not mean anything at all, 'and I said so'. This sounds arrogant today but I felt I had not done myself justice – hence the anger.

'I just can't answer deep philosophical questions about education in forty-five minutes. Some were questions I had thought about a lot . . . my brain doesn't work like that'. Perhaps the two or three long essays I had written during the year – on the function of the school in society, on education in France and on the future of education, helped to pull me through. These at least had had educative value for me as a student. When, ten years on, the Education Department at Leicester University College was initiated, the senate was persuaded to waive any final written three-hour paper examination, following the example set by Helen Wodehouse at Bristol in the 1930s.

So ended my year at the Institute – not with a bang but a whimper.

PARIS IN THE SPRING

I must not omit work in two special groups which contributed to the store of positive experience. The first of these consisted of about a dozen 'mature' students from the dominions – Australia, New Zealand, Canada and South Africa – for whom a special visit to France was arranged in April 1938. These were experienced teachers and educators, spending a full year on secondment at the Institute as overseas 'Fellows' – a scheme which had got under way in 1935. Fred Clarke – the Institute director – was originally appointed as 'Adviser' to these students. I am not sure how I managed to attach myself to this group, but I did. Our leader was Reinhold Schairer, and no more enthusiastic, committed guide, philosopher and friend could be imagined. To stay in Paris in the spring was itself delightful, but this was also a great moment in French politics. A Popular Front government, under Léon Blum, held sway, as it turned out all too briefly. One could not but be aware of the feelings of hope and buoyancy this generated among the people. On the other hand the international situation was worsening, almost daily – as Hitler's increasingly aggressive acts were ineffectually opposed by the democracies. The atmosphere was a great deal more tense than in London. 'Everyone is very panic stricken here', I wrote from Paris. 'We were at the Ministry of Education again today; the Secretary to the Minister told us that it was expected in official circles in France that war would come next week, or anyway in three months.' Everyone in Paris talked of politics and of the war to come – 'the taxi drivers, the people we meet – while I write this I can hear the hotel staff talking'. The Secretary to the Minister had said he would look after me if I came to France – with an expeditionary force, presumably! He was only thirty-two himself, the Minister thirty-four.

At a moment of crisis when Hitler was about to march un-opposed into Austria, Schairer spent hours on the phone maintaining contacts with resistance groupings and individuals in Germany, and at large on the continent. I realise now that he was acting as Carl Goerdeler's confidant and representative in England, sometimes negotiating with the Foreign Office on his behalf. Goerdeler was head of the German 'Widerstand' and chosen to act as Chancellor in the event of a successful army coup, now being planned. This is explained by Klemens von Klemperer in his *German Resistance against Hitler* (1992) where Schairer figures as an 'inveterate activist' on behalf of the German opposition and as Goerdeler's 'personal representative' in England. I later found that Goerdeler was in Paris and that Schairer had arranged contacts for him. At this crucial moment there was always the *hope* that the British government would stand firm, and draw the line somewhere, though the Foreign Secretary, Eden, had resigned in despair a few days earlier. Speeches by his successor Lord Halifax, and Sir John Simon, Chancellor of the Exchequer, were anxiously followed on the radio by Schairer and our party. We felt closely in touch with the developing crisis in Europe during that spring of 1938.

Against this ominous background there could still be useful work; certain visits stood out. The first was to an open-air mixed elementary school in the Paris suburbs, erected by a socialist municipality, Suresnes. At the time 'open-air' schooling enjoyed a considerable vogue, in both France and England, as the key, some thought, to a healthy life. The architectural design of the

French school was modern, money had not been spared, and for me 'the impression given by the whole school was one of extraordinary beauty and gaiety'. There were many trees around which the buildings were patterned. These comprised a main building – refectory, gym room, resting rooms – and classrooms arranged in the form of a circle, each a separate entity surrounded by lawns and trees. Their sliding walls opened completely on three sides and they were heated by warm air, so that, even on the coldest days, the children could work in the open air. There was a small swimming pool, where children bathed naked, and well-equipped medical rooms. Perhaps the outstanding feature of the school was the classroom for mental deficients (the term in use in those days) placed at the centre of the school and around which the other classrooms radiated. It was 'the best equipped classroom, full of flowers, models and paintings', but to me the whole school expressed love for children 'and a real belief in their rights'. It is only fair to add that this school contrasted strongly with others we saw. It was a vision of a possible future – the product of a local community initiative, all the more poignant in the shadow of the barbarism engulfing Europe.

Another noteworthy visit was to the famous 'L'Ecole de l'Ermitage' in Brussels (known internationally as The Hermitage). Founded by the doctor Ovide Decroly before the first world war, this then acted as a focus for 'the New Education' in Belgium and, indeed, on the continent generally. In the 1930s the Decroly 'method', which stressed the child's independent activity and full participation in a cohesive programme based on 'centres of interest', was as well-known and influential as that of Montessori, if radically different in approach. Decroly had died in 1932 but six years on, this school, originally taking only infant and primary children, now ran a full secondary course retaining many of Decroly's principles and procedures. The visit was memorable in that it introduced us to a modern school embodying systematic but 'progressive' principles. Our visit was celebrated by the pupils with a play performed in English, 'Thirty Minutes in a Street', by Beatrice

Mayor. This school (and movement) still continues in Brussels and, I believe, continues to flourish. The procedures characterising it contrasted sharply with the strict formality typical of the French elementary schools and lycées we had visited.

The third visit was of a rather different order. This was to a college for apprentice chefs in Paris – food being a matter taken extremely seriously by the French. The visit consisted solely, if I remember right, in partaking of the most succulent lunch – and the lengthiest (twelve courses) I have ever been offered – prepared, cooked and served by the students. Each course was accompanied by an appropriate wine, concluding with champagne. We tottered out into the late afternoon sunshine agreeing unanimously that this had been the best school visit we had ever made or would be likely to experience in the near future.

NORTHERN EXPOSURE

I was also assigned to a group concerned with the administration of schools. The group was taken under the wing of the Chief Education Officer for Ealing, an enlightened administrator, unusually a member of the New Education Fellowship. We travelled regularly to his base for meetings with the staff but, in all honesty, I cannot say that much was achieved. However it was an addition to my core teaching skills and I had the great good fortune – a fortnight after my year's course ended – to go to Chesterfield to learn from its remarkable director of education, H.G. Stead.

A family connection came in here. Stead, who had worked closely with my father on Education for Citizenship projects, had a national reputation as a creative thinker and innovator in the field of popular education. His first book, *Full Stature* (1936), presenting a clear and enlightened perspective for the future, was succeeded during the war by two more which had a considerable impact: *Modern School Organisation* (1941) and *The Education of a Community* (1942). Chesterfield was then a 'Part III' local authority, its responsibilities confined to the elementary schools in and around the city and attended by most local children. Stead was to give his life to further educational reform in the early years of the Second World War, testing himself beyond the limit; he died in 1943. Although crippled in the Great War he continued his work throughout the country and was in strong demand as a speaker. He insisted on being driven everywhere, often in a motor cycle side car over potholed roads, to meet audiences in remote villages and distant army defence emplacements. His own teaching career had begun in 1906, aged 18, with 70 Standard IV children in his class. Things had improved during the ensuing thirty years, but less rapidly and much less thoroughly than he would have wished. Stead was intent on speeding matters up, and had devised ways of securing his aim.

On this stretch of my training I attended Council meetings, met and talked with councillors and administrators as well as teachers, did the round of absentee pupils with the attendance officer (still known as the 'Board Man') and learned to be wary of ferocious dogs in back streets. Stead's assistants involved me in various ongoing projects – such as choosing the best adapted furniture for a new open air school – while whole days were spent visiting and learning how educational problems were often peculiar to certain schools and so each required individual solutions. Here I found the teachers always friendly and encouraging, quite different, as I noted at the time, from the staff of the City of London school – though the significance of that reference is long since lost to mind.

The Chesterfield set-up provided a view of a local 'system' of education, democratically controlled through elected councillors and their officials. Several of Stead's assistants, who were a lively group, went on to senior appointments elsewhere over the years. Building on Stead's work in the 1930s, Chesterfield later developed a variety of post-primary schools offering different opportunities but open to all. The Chesterfield system then seemed to operate like one large family in which each cooperated with all. Part III authorities were abolished under the 1944 Education Act, though some, like Chesterfield itself, continued in much the same way as 'excepted districts'. The system I observed in 1938 highlighted the advantages of the small authority – as well as the crucial role of local organisation and responsibility in the development, and oversight, of a cohesive school system.

So the weeks in Chesterfield rounded off my first period of training as a teacher – in the event not to be resumed for some seven years.

LABOUR'S EDUCATION ADVISORY COMMITTEE

In December 1937, the Labour Party, preparing for an election that would have to be held before June 1940, set up six committees to advise on policy. These covered health, housing and planning, rating, the rent act, electricity, but the priority was education. For reasons not altogether clear to my memory, I was one of the 25 MPs and others appointed to frame 'a comprehensive statement on education policy'. As a member of the University Labour Federation (ULF) I was automatically a member of the Labour Party, as well as the Communist Party. That this arrangement prevailed was apparently because Anthony Greenwood, as a student at Oxford, had persuaded his father – Arthur Greenwood, then a member of the executive committee – that to exclude student communists would be unwise.

The chairman of the new Education Advisory Committee was Morgan Jones who, having served as Parliamentary Secretary to the Board of Education in both the inter-war (minority) Labour administrations, was the senior 'educationalist' in the party. Among the MPs on it were J. Chuter Ede (to become Parliamentary Secretary to the Board of Education during the Second World War, later Home Secretary), George Tomlinson (Minister of Education 1947-51), Reginald Sorenson, H.B. Lees-Smith and W.G. Cove, the once fiery ex-president of the National Union of Teachers. Other members included Michael Stewart (Secretary of State for Education and Science in 1964-65, then Foreign Secretary), and from the National Union of Teachers, now making an impact, came W.H. Spikes, a grammar school teacher who was a consistent and committed supporter of comprehensive education, and Elsie Parker, president of the union 1937-38. There were also two representatives from the National Association of Labour Teachers and, shortly, four from the New Fabian Research Bureau, emerging as the leading Labour think-tank (Michael Stewart was one of these). A key member was R.H. Tawney who had very successfully master-minded Labour's education policy in the 1920s, and, as secretary, the very committed, experienced and effective Barbara Drake. I was asked, in effect, to act as her 'assistant secretary' (minute taker and general dogsbody). So far as I remember, I took this job on willingly.

As it turned out it was a joy working with Barbara. A niece of Beatrice Webb's, she was a small lady of boundless energy and much charm. Married to a wealthy solicitor she lived in a large, very comfortable house on Campden Hill. Here one met all kinds of unusual people. I recall George Catlin (Shirley Williams' father) for one, but notably broods of Meinetzhagens. Barbara was the daughter of Georgina Potter (Beatrice Webb's sister) and David Meinetzhagen, one of ten children. A very hard working and committed socialist, Barbara was politically on the left of the party. Her work for women trade unionists is well known, but she was in 1938 also a member of the Labour major-ity on the London County Council and a leading member of its education committee. Indeed she was one of those who, already in 1934, had committed the LCC to principles of comprehensive education.

The committee gathered regularly in the dim recesses of the House of Commons, at meetings conducted with due decorum. But one encounter on the way to a meeting remains vividly in mind – with Tawney, as we emerged from the tube station at Westminster. It was a critical moment in international affairs, with a Tory majority backing Chamber-lain's policy of appeasement, and as we approached the Commons Tawney quietly observed that perhaps the best parliamentarian had been Guy Fawkes. Such sentiments were not expressed in committee. This in fact met fourteen times between February 1938 and February 1940 (the last which I attended) and of course there were sub-committees as well. It did a job which, if scarcely revolutionary, was probably important at that time. One item of perhaps historical importance was carried through – a policy recommendation in favour of endorsing the single (multilateral) school as 'immediate practical policy'. This was, in fact, my first involvement with the issue of comprehensive secondary education.

In the summer of 1938 Morgan Jones, who had chaired the first four meetings, fell ill, and was replaced by the loveable George Tomlinson for whom Chuter Ede substituted on occasions, (except the one when a collective apology came from the MPs, required for a debate on the education estimates, and R.H. Tawney took over).

For me, attendance provided an unusual opportunity to see something of policy making from the inside, even to assist in it, since I was given a number of opportunities to undertake work. In May 1938 I was added to a policy sub-committee to discuss priorities, comprising Tawney, Tomlinson, Spikes, Barbara and two others. Only a record of the first meeting has survived, but this records that I was deputed both to prepare a memo on the training of teachers and to condense a lengthy and very effective statement by the University Labour Federation on university policy, prepared for the NUS congress that year. A month later I was appointed convenor of two sub-committees, one on the training of teachers (with Michael Stewart, Spikes and Barbara), and one on university policy (with these again, together with my Cambridge supervisor, Lionel Elvin, also a member of the committee). Needless to say, I was somewhat busy during this period.

As well as my work at the Commons, I was involved with the NUS and a member of a newly founded committee for students of education. Another project undertaken was to draft a pamphlet on teacher training for the New Fabian Research Bureau. A lengthy letter from Tawney, as illegible as customary, found the result 'interesting and to the point', and suggested a discussion. On the other hand a note about the reaction of my father indicates a feeling on his part that I was taking on too much for my age – maybe also working too hard. I concentrated on my programme both at home in Manchester and at the cottage my father rented for years from the National Trust – Hellsgarth, at the head of Langdale, the valley G.M. Trevelyan did so much to preserve (and to which my family is devoted). I also completed drafts for the Labour committee, sending off nineteen pages of typescript to Barbara Drake who responded, somewhat overwhelmed, 'I can't keep up with you'. However she had more work to hand on next time we met. As to what emerged for the Labour Party from all this, the teacher training pamphlet certainly never saw publication and what I chiefly recall is the emphasis on the *multilateral* school.

The term emerged only after intensive discussion and the policy implied was unanimously agreed – but was set aside in post-war years by George Tomlinson (who had duly voted for it in 1938), in succession to Ellen Wilkinson, the first Labour Minister of Education in 1945. Another memory is of the advisory committee's necessary switch of concern in 1939 towards such impending matters as evacuation plans and the immense problems now facing the London school system. The Labour Party never appointed a post-war advisory committee, I think I am right in saying, and the more's the pity so far as a sound policy for education and adherence to it went. Barbara Drake died in 1963, apparently leaving no papers. I never saw her again after the war but count myself lucky to have had the opportunity to work for her. Modest and unassuming however capable, she put all her energy into the work in hand to which she was entirely committed – as did so many others who set Labour objectives and, after the war, created a new school system for London's children.

THE NATIONAL UNION OF STUDENTS

At the Institute I was elected to the post of NUS secretary,

which meant keeping in touch with NUS activities and especially with enquiries of the kind which we had undertaken at
Cambridge and were now also underway in most universities,
enquiries reflecting a concern with educational teaching standards. Then in July 1938, as my training year ended, I was
elected Vice-President of the Union (one of four), and a year
later President, with a term which ran beyond the outbreak of
war – to November 1940. For these two years I was occupied
full-time with NUS work, even though I had been called up to
the army. By 1938 my own interest in educational affairs – and
that of the union – was merging directly with political concerns.
It could not be otherwise, given the growing threat of Nazi
Germany, and inadequacy of the British government's policy of
appeasement, which seemed to parallel the past failures to rectify
social and economic ills.

I do not regret a moment of the time I spent in the 'student
movement' of the 1930s. At times matters became fraught,
indeed the summer of 1940 saw a determined, almost successful,
attempt to close the NUS down for the duration. Policies were
too radical, it was said, and the kind of activities the NUS
planned to pursue – widespread discussion of issues seen as
important, determined action to maintain the universities as
functioning entities – were deemed inappropriate in wartime. So
there was a really tough battle to secure survival. All this can be
seen, in retrospect, as educative – or anyway formative. Many of
those involved bonded in close friendships, which have remained
green throughout life, among those who survived. Of those who
did not I remember particularly John Symonds, a lawyer (a
major in the Airborne Division, killed at Arnhem), and Ram
Nahum, a brilliant young physicist, killed by the only bomb to
fall on Cambridge during the war. Freddie Vickers, also there at
the time, survived injury with great courage. Margot Gale (later
Kettle) became an indispensable secretary of the NUS, working
in Cambridge. James Klugmann was a Cambridge friend promi-
nent in the student leadership organised through the University
Labour Federation and the Communist Party; so were George
and Betty Matthews, Jack Cohen and Arnold Kettle, among

many others who debated key issues and planned wartime work.

With the outbreak of war in September 1939 I suddenly found myself, in effect, acting as secretary of the NUS as well as its president. This was because the actual secretary, R. Nunn May, and others of the full-time staff, simply decamped to take up appointments at the Ministry of Information, newly established in London University's Senate House – a few hundred yards from our headquarters, in Endsleigh Street. This had been arranged by Ivison Macadam – the original founder of the NUS and now a trustee – who had himself been recruited from his job as Secretary of Chatham House to a leading position in the new ministry. Naturally May's departure left a gap which, fortunately, I was able to fill.

In the normal course of events, after completing the Institute course and gaining its diploma, I should have gone straight into a career in teaching. But as a result of my work with the NUS, I was asked to write a book, detailing student enquiries into university education. The NUS would sponsor the project, finance it and provide all the secretarial help required. Having duly agreed in the summer of 1938, I started on this project. A year later, with extensive work still incomplete, and as I assumed the post of President, I had little choice other than to concentrate time and energies on the NUS.

Initially I prepared an ambitious synopsis for the book (which still survives) while the general secretary of the NUS wrote to a number of institutions seeking data on the social origins of their students amongst other related matters. Open-ended questionnaires were also sent to selected lecturers and professors, resulting in lengthy and thoughtful responses; from, among others, Bonamy Dobrée and L.C. Knights, both becoming well known for their critical thinking about universities. Margery Fry, then a member of the University Grants Committee and an innovative thinker as well as a very charming person, suggested I undertake a systematic sampling of student opinion in certain faculties – the NUS and various student unions set this up. In addition a considerable number of more or less distinguished university teachers agreed to an interview – largely people identified by the NUS, or universities, as innovative, or 'critical'. At Birmingham, three gave their time generously. Sargant Florence, responsible for new approaches in the Faculty of Commerce, George Thomson, newly appointed from Cambridge as Professor of Greek, and in particular Raymond Priestley, the energetic and sympathetic Vice-Chancellor. At Cambridge help came from C.P. Snow, then teaching in the science faculty. At Oxford Christopher Hill, who had recently taught history at Cardiff, gave full details of problems there, while A.J.P. Taylor was likewise generous with time and advice (but not, later, in his reception of the book!). Patrick Blackett, Professor of Physics at Manchester, and R.A.C. Oliver, Professor of Education there, were both ready to talk – but Manchester was home ground. Several other education professors and lecturers were interviewed, notably a group at Exeter which included J.W. Tibble, later to become the first professor of education at Leicester. This group outlined a pattern, or structure, of psychological and medical as well as academic support for students far ahead of its time.

This project gave me plenty to do during the academic year 1938-39 but it remained unfinished in the summer of 1939 when I was elected president of NUS. At this point my father urged me to complete the work during my year of office but, with the outbreak of war, it became obvious that neither the NUS nor I would be able to complete the project as originally planned.

There were other alternatives – instead of an official, weighty publication on behalf of NUS, the material gathered might be used for what could only be a personal statement. When possible, in the new circumstances, I turned my mind to this project which was finally (in 1943) to surface as 'A Student's View of the Universities' rather than the originally projected title of 'The Students' View . . .'.

My work for the NUS continued to escalate, partly due to the increasing involvement of the more articulate students in the critique of university education, and of a determination to link more closely with the emerging youth movement outside of university, concerned to improve the working and living conditions of young people. There was also a growing, official, involvement with the international youth and student movement, which found expression in the representation of the NUS at the second World Youth Congress held at Vassar in the United States in 1938. The NUS sponsored an official student delegation to Republican Spain and began to work with the World Student Association, based in Paris. This attracted student organisations from around the world (for instance, India, Indonesia and China), by contrast with CIE (Confederation Internationale des Étudiants), established after World War One, confined only to official unions in Europe and by now virtually defunct.

Two of the main events of the academic year 1938-1939 with which the NUS was connected, were the National Youth Hearing and the National Parliament of Youth, held in January and March 1939 respectively. The first was concerned to highlight the conditions of youth generally, culminating in a campaign for a Youth Charter comprising a set of principles to govern the conditions of life and work of young people. The second (the Youth Parliament) attracted over a thousand representatives from youth organisations all over the country. Here the NUS presented an Education 'Reform' Bill which outlined a plan for full-time compulsory education for all children up to the age of sixteen, a single (unified) code of administration (in place of the then existing separate codes for elementary and secondary education), the provision of more generous maintenance grants for pupils remaining at school after fourteen, and other measures relating both to schools and universities. These events received considerable publicity in the national press and paved the way for new levels of cooperation between the leading national student organisations and those of young people generally. Both involved me in a good deal of work researching the issues involved in our submission on the conditions of students (for the Youth Hearing), and in the precise formulations of the clauses of the Bill presented to the Youth Parliament.

The general direction of these activities was, in a sense, crystallised at the annual NUS congress held at Easter 1939. Here Reinhold Schairer, an invited speaker, had an electrical effect:

'The isolation of the universities as institutions for social advancement must go', he proclaimed, 'and there must be a return to the ideal of Condorcet who saw in them the living centre of the whole learning of the nation'. At this congress, commissions worked on the means by which university students could assist in the solution of pressing social problems both nationally and locally, and, in particular, transform universities, in President Roosevelt's memorable words, into 'fortresses of democracy'.

There was, at this time, a growing determination among students not to allow universities, in any part of the world, to fall victim to fascist ideology and control – as had happened in Germany where resistance to Nazism had been slight. Encouragement of this approach was derived from the establishment of workers' universities in Republican Spain while the war was still under way and by the Chinese Eighth Route Army during the struggle against the Japanese. This was one aspect of the politicisation of that generation of students.

Throughout 1938-1939, as I gathered material for the NUS book and took part in these activities, international tension intensified. It was against this background that the NUS sent a strong delegation, with other student organisations (including the Federation of University Conservative and Unionist Associations) to the conference organised by the World Student Association in Paris in August 1939. Celebrating the 150th anniversary of the French Revolution, this conference (organised by my friend James Klugmann, Secretary of WSA), had a wide range of distinguished sponsors including Lloyd George, Gilbert Murray, H.G. Wells, J.S.B. Stopford and Albert Einstein; the main speakers included Dr Wellington Koo (Chinese Ambassador to France), Pablo Neruda the Chilean poet, and Ernest Simon (my father). I was invited to act as the leader of the British delegation, which included representatives from all the main national student organisations.

This, then, was a last fling before the curtain came down. Paris provided an ideal setting for such a meeting, which was attended by delegates from China, Republican Spain, Indonesia, India, the

United States and many European countries not yet under the heel of fascism. The conference itself was remarkable for the efficiency of its organisation, the sense of solidarity, cultural diversity, and comradeship in the common struggle. My father (it fell to my lot to act as chairman for his address) was deeply impressed. On return he wrote a fine article, published in the *Manchester Guardian* late in August 1939, just a few days before the cataclysmic events which heralded the outbreak of the Second World War, giving a very positive assessment of the conference. As the students dispersed, a few of us took off for a few days holiday in Brittany. As we returned to England, news of the German-Soviet pact was broadcast to the world; the long drawn out British negotiations with the Soviet Union had fallen through. A few days later German troops launched their all-out assault on Poland.

It was at this point that Nunn May, the experienced General Secretary of the NUS (and ex-President), decamped to the Ministry of Information. A temporary replacement was found, but she had no experience, nor any knowledge of the various activities on which the union was engaged. As Vice-President and President Elect, working full-time on the NUS book (and living next door), I found myself in practice taking over these activities and in more or less full-time work. Everyone concerned wanted me to continue with this job rather than volunteer for the armed services and, in the circumstances, this seemed the right decision.

There were two main foci for future student work. First, what we saw as a necessary defence of the universities against depredations of any kind; second, encouragement of free discussion of economic, social and political issues and, especially, the role of the universities in facilitating these. In effect, this was to further the work of the last two or three congresses and the first, defence of the universities, seemed the most immediately important.

The war though was taking its toll. Arbitrary commandeering of buildings, evacuations, and the reduction of income and financial assistance generally (both to universities and students) quickly seemed to threaten the whole system of higher education. At the October meeting of the NUS Council (the union's governing body) there was unanimous support for effective action 'to prevent university education falling a victim to the present crisis'. First, there must be a 'thorough investigation' of the position, then 'action on a national scale'.

In January 1940 the NUS published a short pamphlet 'Defend the Universities' which I drafted on the basis of information received. It argued for an increase in Treasury grant to offset reduction in income and increased costs, and also for the 'postponement of military service for all students who have successfully completed one year of study'. Both lines of action, recommended by Council, had been agreed unanimously by the Executive Committee. Both were based on the broad concept of the function of the university worked out at NUS congresses – as the learning centres of the nation – and widely accepted by the student body at large and by representative student unions.

The pamphlet received widespread and sympathetic coverage in the press (e.g *The Times, Manchester Guardian, Sunday Times, Observer*). A campaign was developed around this programme, while I had my first experience of leading a deputation to the Ministry of Labour to argue the case. Promises were made to consider seriously our points so that, together with other forms of activity, we began to feel that we were making an impact. Our stand, however, and degree of commitment, led to a negative reaction in some quarters. I personally came under considerable pressure from Tory MPs who felt our policy relating to military service was wrong and should be amended. At this stage Ivison Macadam, still leading trustee of the NUS, though now an official of the Ministry of Information, began to be concerned about the general direction of our activities, though he had, of course, no position on the executive committee.

The second main line of action at this time, following up former work, was the promotion of widespread discussion among students of leading economic, social and political issues of the day, focusing especially on the role of universities in the existing critical situation. In hand was an ambitious project – the organisation of a 'British Student Congress' at Leeds University for a full week in March 1940. This was, of course, still the period of 'phoney' war – British troops had yet to be seriously engaged in combat – and, although certain London colleges had been evacuated, the impetus of student activities engendered over the past two or three years had been maintained and developed: but the week long congress was a new venture. Organised by the NUS, in consultation with the British Universities League of Nations Society, the International Student Service (ISS), the Student Christian Movement, and the three political student organisations – the University Labour Federation, the Liberals and the Conservatives – it aimed to provide a forum for all views within the student movement. It was symptomatic of the time that student Conservatives fully participated in all these activities, including aid for Spain.

Preparing for the congress ensued, with discussions, forums and debates held throughout the universities. At Manchester University, for instance, twenty faculty, religious and political societies took part in organised discussions on the congress issues; at Nottingham a local congress was planned to precede the national congress – it was even claimed that *all* Nottingham students were drawn into these discussions. At Cambridge also, political and faculty societies held preliminary discussions, the aim being to send a representative group of students to the congress.

The programme of the congress was agreed by all the national participating organisations. I remember one preparatory session held by the ISS, with Sir Walter Moberly (the Chairman of both the University Grants Committee and the ISS) in the chair and the historian, Lewis Namier, present. The latter could scarcely contain himself at the thought that the students were to vote a resolution on India after only three days' discussion; but here Moberly's avuncular support carried the day. When under criticism for this and other matters, incidentally, the NUS (and I personally) received strong, if informal, support from Fred Clarke, Principal of the London University Institute of Education.

The congress met under the auspices of a number of patrons – friends of the student movement. These included Ernest Barker, Carr-Saunders (then Director of the London School of Economics), A.D. Lindsay (Master of Balliol College, Oxford), and the Vice-Chancellors of Leeds, Birmingham and Manchester universities. The main speaker (and the only one other than students) was H.G. Wells – and his message did not go down well with the assembled students. Over 600 attended – by far the largest number to attend a congress up to that date – though those organised later in the war drew well over 1000.

The congress worked in commissions. For the first three days it considered international, social and political issues; then moved on to the problems of universities and colleges. It concluded with the adoption of a charter of student rights and responsibilities. In view of the radical nature of the resolutions passed, usually by huge majorities, it is worth recording an analysis based on questionnaires filled in by 332 delegates. Of these 73 per cent came from 'secondary' (i.e. 'grammar') schools, 27 per cent from public schools. Subjects of study covered all the main fields relatively equally. Forty per cent belonged to 'one or other' student society, but 60 per cent to none. In the words of the report, 'those who came to learn, and they were the majority of the Congress, found their ideas changing and were able to free themselves from their fixed ideas and conceptions'. However that may be, the level of discussion in the various commissions was extraordinarily high, the degree of unanimity remarkable.

The congress passed resolutions demanding economic as well as political equality (by 378 to 19), condemned the system of private production for profit and called for a planned economy (by 416 to 9). Equal opportunities in education and 'a total reorganisation of the Board of Education and of the systems of training and remuneration of teachers' were called for (by 382 to 12). Congress also condemned the arrest of one hundred student leaders of the All India Student Federation (by 426 to 2), demanded immediate independence for India, and pledged 'full support for their struggle for freedom' (382 to 26); imperialism and the colonial system were condemned (in a long resolution), by 362 to 23. There were, of course, other resolutions but they attracted less attention. 'The remarkable unanimity of the Congress on these questions', runs the report, 'is a striking indication of the direction in which the thoughts and ideas of young people are turning. These decisions were not snap decisions. They were taken after hearing all points of view, and much information on the subjects under discussion'.

The congress also passed a resolution (by 281 votes to 150, with 48 abstentions), stating that the continuance of the war was against the interests of every country and that it was the duty of students in all countries to work to end it. Here two things must be remembered: the war was still 'phoney' and Chamberlain remained Prime Minister, with Halifax as Foreign Secretary, heading a Conservative government of the order dominant throughout most of the 1930s. There was alienation, scepticism and much mistrust in student circles, including deep suspicion that the intention was to switch the war against the Soviet Union – or side with Hitler to crown the appeasement policy.

It is difficult to convey the atmosphere of the congress, but one finding of the report, concerning curricula, may help. The two extreme concepts – that of a strictly technical education on the one hand, and that which makes a fetish of 'knowledge for its own sake' on the other – were both rejected: 'Between these two extremes the student fails to get any understanding of the world in which he lives or the relation of his studies to the social needs of the time.' This engenders a 'feeling of frustration and aimlessness amongst many students and the degeneration of culture into something pedantic and esoteric. The universities should be centres of a live and growing culture which draws on the experience of the past for the purposes of the present and the future and is at the disposal of the whole people'.

Resolutions covered a wide field. Presaging Robbins, congress resolved that university education should be available to all with 'the necessary ability'; that universities should be democratised by means of student representation on all governing bodies, and through 'proper consultation with the representatives of the students on all matters affecting the students'. Curricula which are 'abstract, divorced from other spheres of human activity and knowledge, and unrelated to social needs' should give way to curricula 'which relate each particular "subject" to all the other spheres of knowledge, which show the development of the "subject" in relation to developing social and intellectual conditions, and which make clear its relevance to the needs of society'. A 'radical change' in methods of teaching was called for 'in order to develop the full capabilities and critical faculties of students' – more seminars and discussion groups, individual tuition, 'and very much less reliance on lectures'. The examination system also needed change. A whole programme was worked out to bring universities much more closely in contact with youth, other sections of society, and the people generally. It was felt that the composition of universities should correspond more closely to that of society generally; with a far higher proportion of working-class students recruited and financed, and mature students with experience of work in industry and the professions.

The resolutions passed at the congress, incidentally, did not commit the NUS, only those present. Policy was the preserve of the NUS Council on which all affiliated unions were represented, which met three times a year. There was, however, a dramatic outcome to the Leeds Congress. A few weeks later a new General Secretary was appointed to ensure the union continued to function effectively – Margot Gale – but the NUS trustees objected. I joined the Army a fortnight later but still continued to function as President as best I could. A serious attempt was made by the trustees and two or three Executive Committee members to take over the NUS, by *coup d'état* as it were, in order to close it down for the duration. This move was mounted shortly after the German breakthrough in France, followed by the debacle at Dunkirk.

The technique adopted by the rogue members was to issue a telegram, claiming to be official, from NUS headquarters announcing that an imminent Council meeting had been cancelled and the NUS organisation taken over by the trustees.

The plan failed. On hearing of it (at my army base in Dorchester – I was a private in the Dorset regiment) I was able to instruct the secretary to send out counter-telegrams announcing that the council was to take place as planned. All this happened just a day or two before the proposed meeting and naturally lead to considerable confusion, but in the event the meeting took place as planned and I managed to get leave to be present. This meeting elected the next year's officers, thus validating the action of the President and Secretary in convening it, and called for the resignation of the trustees.

Over the summer this particular battle continued, but the NUS survived. At the November council in Manchester, when I relinquished the presidency, the Sheffield council decisions were validated – but only narrowly. So, in a peace-making gesture the officers elected in Sheffield resigned en masse, only (bar one) to be re-elected. More important, new trustees were elected who supported the NUS (notably, Carr-Saunders, Principal of the London School of Economics), relegating Nunn May and others who had participated in the attempt at closure. From this point the NUS went from strength to strength.

In *The Rise of the Student Estate in Britain* (Ashby and Anderson 1970), a chapter is devoted to the NUS in the 1920s and 1930s up to the Leeds Congress and wartime consolidation. This is seen as the background to 'the flowering of the student estate' following World War Two. In 1941, 1942 and again in 1943 NUS congresses were attended by more than one thousand students. Training colleges and technical colleges were now admitted into full membership – a project that began in my time (1939-40). Representatives of the NUS engaged in regular consultation with members of parliament, government departments, the Association of University Teachers, the National Union of Teachers, and the University Grants Committee. All this had its inception in the late 1930s. In 1944 the NUS published a major report on the reform of higher education, described by Ashby as 'the first considered manifesto from the student estate, a corporate statement agreed after drafts had been circulated to all constituent organisations of NUS'. Had the

NUS been closed down, as the trustees wanted in 1940, none of this could have been achieved.

There is no question that all this was a fascinating and educative experience for me personally. But, to round matters off on a more personal note, the manuscript of *A Student's View of the Universities* was completed during 1940-41 and seen by my father in the press, being finally published by Longmans, Green, late in 1943. I received my copy in south Italy, having reached there after serving with the First Army in Algeria and Tunisia. Also in February 1941 I married Joan Peel who had recently joined Harold Dent, editor of the *Times Educational Supplement*, at his invitation, as an assistant. The two comprised the entire journalistic staff for the next two years, a period when, as a later editor of the journal put it, 'Dent drove himself on all cylinders to take a lead in policy-making', during 'war-torn years' which must rank as 'the most exhilarating, demanding and influential in the paper's history'. My wife's position meant that although I was in the Army – and abroad for long periods – I was never out of touch with wartime educational developments, not least the battle to ensure a worthwhile Education Act, to settle the future organisation of the nation's schools.

3

TEACHING IN MANCHESTER AND SALFORD, 1945-50

Called up to the army in May 1940 I was granted early release as a trained teacher just before Christmas 1945 – a period mostly spent with a kind of 'private army' known as Phantom. Formed during the Dunkirk debacle its main job was to keep the army commander informed directly, by mobile patrols equipped with shortwave transmitters, of all observable troop movements and developments in the area for which he was responsible. Everything depended on reliable, often long distance, communications operating effectively, and as a signals officer this was my main responsibility. Events took me first to Algeria and Tunisia with the First Army, then to Italy with the Eighth, and finally to France, Belgium and Germany with the Canadian army.

Among the rather unusual people in this unit were David Niven, with whose squadron I spent a hilarious training week in Devonshire; the political philosopher Michael Oakeshott who had taught me at Cambridge; and two Astors (Jakie and Michael – very different characters). Hugh Fraser, later a maverick Tory MP, commanded our squadron in Italy; the actor Hugh ('Tam') Williams was good company there, Peregrine Worsthorne another matter. Our founder, the remarkable General Hopkinson, was sadly killed at Taranto when commanding the First Airborne Division, with whom we made the crossing from Africa.

Generally speaking the unit did a good job on various fronts during the war and I was lucky to be part of it. Annual reunions were still well attended into the late 1990s as most of us reached our eighties: the bonds formed in wartime experience hold. I was, of course, also lucky to survive.

The only activities of a directly educational nature were participation in the ABCA (Army Bureau of Current Affairs) lectures, seminars and discussions, undertaken when unemployed in Africa and Italy, and, later, when waiting in England for the Second Front. These were taken reasonably seriously and were generally enjoyable. A course at Coleg Harlech (an ABCA centre) introduced me effectively into modern techniques of adult education.

I returned from army life to my wife, and two small boys, and settled in Manchester. On demobilisation in December 1945 I was aged 30 years, 9 months. 'At long last begin my professional career', I noted in January 1946. Manchester was prepared to take me on as a teacher, and its chief inspector, W.T. Stephenson, took me under his wing to help with my induction. This was a result of family influence, I suppose, but much the same was done for Further Education and Training Students (FETS) on completing terms of conscription later. It was, after all, over seven years since I had undertaken my teacher training.

The object, of course, was to become thoroughly involved with the 'real' problems of education – teaching and learning in proper public schools maintained by local education authorities. Like many ex-servicemen, I was fuelled by a sense of urgency; if the army years had not been wasted there had been a long delay for one with a clear idea of chosen work by 1939. Moreover the massive Labour victory at the polls in July 1945 clearly opened a new perspective in terms of social change, while allied victory in the Far East, together with the founding of the United Nations, held a fresh promise for international relations. The successful passage of the 1944 Education Act, preceded by years of discussion, seemed to offer a new beginning in education. Whatever lay ahead, the years 1946 and 1947 when my teaching career was in its infancy, I saw as years of hope.

I spent my first term's work teaching at Yew Tree 'selective central' school at Wythenshawe, Manchester's satellite city. The next (summer) term Stephenson shifted me to an 'all-age' (and so still 'elementary') school in the centre of Manchester, Abbott Street. Thereafter I had a full year at a secondary modern school in Openshaw, then Manchester's engineering district. This took me to the summer of 1947. I then applied for, and was appointed as a 'master' at Salford Grammar School, where I spent three years before joining University College, Leicester, as a Lecturer in Education in October 1950.

My first term's teaching at Yew Tree proved stimulating if, in some senses, somewhat chaotic; the harassed, temporary, head-mistress had severe staffing problems. My earliest notes illustrate that I was greatly impressed by colleagues, their keenness on the job and concern for the children's welfare. 'All subjects come up for discussion in the common room, effect of home environment, discipline, individual pupils, organisation of the school, multilateral schools and so on'. Very stimulating, I added, 'All genuinely interested in their work'.

A variety of theoretical issues hit me during my first week at Yew Tree. How far was this school genuinely selective (as it was intended – a 'selective' central school)? By what criteria were the three streams, A, B and C formed? What was, or should be, the role of the head (who spent much of her time filling in forms)? How far was the content of education, and in particular, methods of teaching, appropriate to these particular children? With these and related matters in mind the writings of the classic educators of the past, for instance J.F. Herbart, took on a new immediacy – I already began to feel the necessity of an almost complete *reconstruction* of education.

I will return to these broader issues later. My first term's teaching filled the foreground – a valuable experience thoroughly enjoyed. But Yew Tree was a world away from the grim realities of central Manchester. The building was modern: built in 1937 it was the local show school of its type, designed on the 'open air' principles then popular – which certainly produced a gusty environment! My next assignment, Abbott Street, was very different.

This was an old 'Board School', originally erected in 1875 in the heart of the slum district, north of Albert Square. Still an all-age school (i.e. not yet reorganised on 'Hadow' principles), it catered for children of both sexes from the age of seven to fourteen; the school leaving age was only raised to fifteen in April 1947, a year after I started there. A few, but very few, pupils passed the 11+ to be offered places in grammar schools. The great majority stayed where they were, moving up each year to a higher form, or 'standard', as each class was still labelled in nineteenth century nomenclature. There was one for each annual age group – on emerging from infant school children entered Standard 1. Class teaching was the rule up to and including Standard VII, the 13-14 age group.

The area was a neglected slum, the schools serving it, ancient, run down and overcrowded – particularly those controlled by religious (or voluntary) bodies. I well remember visiting a friend, head of a nearby Catholic school. The school hall housed four classes, each numbering at least forty, separated only by curtains; the school must have been built before the 'class' system developed where different 'classes' were allocated specific rooms, i.e. before about 1875. One reached the school from Abbott Street by Paradise Lane. Beside it flowed (if that is the right word) the malodorous River Irk – bright green in the mornings, yellow in the afternoons. Yet here again were devoted, professional teachers, doing what they could.

My first job at Abbott Street was to take Standard II, all day for a month – thirty children aged 8 'with IQs ranging (probably) from 70 – 120' (as I noted). This was what would now be called a 'mixed ability' or 'unstreamed' class. About seven or eight children could scarcely read. 'Two girls have tremendous casts in their eyes, one has a sore instead of an eye, one girl had toothache, another spat out a bloody tooth during the lesson. Quite a change from Yew Tree'. The head had been there for 26 years, but he was 'quite unable to give me any hints about teaching and left me to get on with the job!'. I kept the children busy, it seemed, with 'reading, writing, talking'; but 'there wasn't much *theory* behind it'. It was the kind of job I had wanted; 'if I find my feet teaching these kids it should be first rate experience'. There was no syllabus. It was for me to concoct one and go ahead with it.

'The time goes quickly!' is the comment ten days later. So far I had focussed on arithmetic, reading and writing, as well as reading to the class, talking, acting, telling stories (some very macabre stories were told by the children), 'even a little singing'. 'Modern' education had hardly penetrated the school – 'the other classes do formal education all day, there is little activity involving movement. No PT. The playground is very small'. Even for the three Rs 'there appear to be no real standards available for the whole school'. There was also a lack of modern reading books. 'I am very ignorant of the educational methods necessary', runs a somewhat naive note, 'but am finding out'. There were 'great divergencies' in the same class, which included 'bright children interested in everything and very keen to learn, and dull ones'. Some of the kids seemed to bear a grudge against the world – as if 'they had been sat on or spoken sharply to for years'. Children were unable to concentrate for long – 'the ideal would be short lessons (half an hour) and plenty of activity', but to achieve this would involve 'a considerable amount of help and experience'.

My fellow teachers at Abbott Street seemed to me highly professional (within the limits of received pedagogical practice at that time), and were to me personally very helpful. On occasions I was able to sit in on their lessons and, by this means, learnt a lot – especially about class management. I have before me as I write a minute-by-minute observational account of a full day's teaching by the highly skilled teacher of Standard III (age 9-10). As the record has a historical interest, in terms of current discussions of pedagogy, an extended excerpt follows:

10.30. After break for milk immediately noticeable that the teacher has complete control of the class; children are on the spot and obey him immediately.

1 Kids say money table all together (40p is three and fourpence, 48p is four shillings, etc., parrot fashion).
2 Through the table again individually. Teacher walks round pointing at children who say the next number. Answers

come quickly.
3   12 times table – all together.
4   12 times table backwards.
5   Clock on board. Starts at a number, goes all round (kids together).
6   Again.
7   Again, individually. One girl gives a wrong answer; he jumps on her heavily and starts again.
8   11 times table – all together.
9   11 times table – backwards.
10 11 times table – individually.

And so on. The class are on their toes throughout. In 15 minutes the teacher has carried out 26 different operations.

There followed a school break of fifteen minutes. At 11.05, mental arithmetic for ten minutes. The teacher formulates problems involving adding, subtracting, multiplying, dividing, with ordinary numbers and sometimes money (pennies, shillings). At 11.15 'take out sum books' (no relaxation of any kind), 'Right, carry on'. Half the class immediately queue beside his desk for corrections, the rest work at their own pace through a textbook, taking up the rough work for correction every three or four sums. In the afternoon, spelling (on a similar system), sentence building – and here some class discussion. After 3 p.m. quiet reading – children called up individually to read to the teacher; at 3.25 all books collected. Till 4 p.m. the class recites six poems they know by heart; 'they seem to enjoy this a good deal', I noted. Then he teaches them another verse of Lochinvar 'getting a certain amount of expression' (from the children). The record ends in capital letters:

1600 END OF DAY. KIDS SAY A PRAYER AND FILE AWAY.

There is a ritual for this too. Here is my record of the end of the morning's work:

'Right places'; all sit (this is the end of the maths lesson described above).

All arrange their desks, each book in right place, he looks rapidly at each desk.

All books collected. He names an individual from each group (of four) who each collects a book and a pencil from the other members of the group; the monitors then collect these and put them away in a cupboard.

'Stand'. All stand. All say prayer (grace).

'Gangways down'. All move out of desks to space between each row.

At his word, all move to form two lines at the door.

At his word, the door is opened and the children file out. All the time he watches them closely and checks the odd child. He never raises his voice, but normally uses a strong voice in the classroom ('It is important', he says, 'to have a stable system').

It may seem odd, but there was much, here, of value to the apprentice teacher of exactly fifty years ago. Class management was a crucial skill without which nothing of any significance could possibly be achieved. The focus on whole class activities – recognition of the social nature of learning – this had value, especially with an unstreamed class. The disciplinary measures – particularly movement into and out of the class – embodied the, by now, long historical experience of the elementary school teacher.

These methods were not designed to encourage enquiring minds and independent initiative – rather the opposite. But they were concerned to ensure conditions for learning – even if, here too, aims were limited. So they formed a base on which new approaches, with wider objectives, might be built – or so, now, it seems to me. Nor were the teachers other than humanistic in relations with their pupils. The head admittedly relied on corporal punishment as the ultimate sanction, but class teachers worked hard and skilfully to improve teaching-learning relations with their pupils.

There is no doubt that I learned a lot about teaching at Abbott

Street, particularly about the need (with 7 and 8 year olds) 'to explain every little thing with extreme simplicity and clarity' (as I put it at the time). On the whole, runs a report on my term's work, 'I learnt about the highly skilled job of class management, a job crammed full of human situations and therefore of human interests, of which the real key is to make each child feel that he/she is wanted and socially useful'. In general 'I constantly felt what an immense amount could be done with these children in the right environment and with a more purposive educational technique. I also felt my own inadequacy in that I myself was not really able to bring out all that was best in them, partly through lack of experience and training, partly because it is the whole school environment that needs changing, but also, and very importantly, because of the lack of a clear lead from the educational world generally on the whole question of basic educational theory and its concrete application in the schools'. Half a century on the problem is still with us.

After the term at Abbott Street I was transferred for a year to a secondary modern school – Varna Street in Openshaw. My teaching here, as noted towards the end of the year, had been 'interesting'. One term was with the leavers' group, where I attempted a more realistic educational content 'but failed to work out adequately group activities and expressive work based on it'. Two terms were spent with a 'B' form of 12 year olds, 'a most pleasant and lively class'. Varna Street still retained the old 'elementary' system of class teaching (one took the same form for all, or most, subjects), in general 'a most illuminating and valuable experience'. The school was well organised, the feeling and tone good, 'the teachers generally enthusiastic and very competent', if 'somewhat traditional in their methods and content'. 'I find my critical faculties somewhat blunted', I noted, 'compared to a year ago'; that is, 'beginning to take traditional work for granted – maybe falling slightly into a rut'. This suggests the power of long-established institutional routine in shaping behaviour and attitudes; or the conservatism inherent in educational institutions in particular.

Arising directly from actual teaching experience in

Manchester schools in 1946 and 1947 were a whole number of theoretical issues which became a focus for study and activity – and discussions at home with my wife Joan, with whom I shared similar educational and political interests. The area that now came to the fore was the technique used to allocate children into discrete 'streams' (A, B and C, etc.) found at both Yew Tree and Varna Street. Early in 1946, soon after starting to teach, there is a note, 'Must learn a lot about intelligence testing as a vital technique for the new education'. But, after some weeks' study, my notes reflect the beginnings of a questioning as to the validity and applicability of intelligence testing, though tests still seemed crucial to serious research into education – a research project designed but not carried through figures as 'a test of intelligence tests'.

So the central focus of my thinking became the need for a transformation of the content of secondary education. To envisage a common, comprehensive, school was to see the 'academic' grammar school approach as arid and subject-centred on the one hand, and to be as critical of the lack of clarity and objective in the senior or new secondary modern schools. Given the return of a Labour government in 1945 an organisational transition to the single school seemed in sight; this was, after all, their agreed policy. But more was needed – an overall reconstruction of educational practice utilising modern methods and techniques; the enhancing of children's disciplined activity, the devising of activities directed to defined and desirable educational ends. Before and during the war practising teachers had consistently taken up professional issues through the unions, but the passage of the 1944 Act redefined educational tasks and this change called for attention from the Left, if anything effective was to be contributed in contemporary educational affairs. Three years' experience teaching in a boys' grammar school contributed to clarifying this train of thought.

Salford Grammar School was a typical urban boys' school – established by the City Council after the 1902 Education Act legitimised spending from the rates in support of secondary education. It was partnered by a parallel girls' school: they were the only publicly maintained schools at secondary level in the city, sponsored by one of the poorest authorities. The school was then situated in Leaf Square, in the centre of the city – a pleasant area then comprising early nineteenth century Georgian red brick buildings – under the headmastership of the progressive and humanistic E.G. Simm.

My main job was to teach English throughout the school from the first form to the sixth, and also economics at sixth form level. Consequently in my last year or two, I spent quite a lot of time with small sixth form classes then characteristic of grammar schools – about eight in each class for English, fewer for economics. One of my economics pupils, a very talented boy, won an Open Scholarship to the London School of Economics, apparently an almost unprecedented event; in celebration the whole school was given a full day's holiday. But I also acted as form-master to each of the three first forms of 11 year-olds and taught English to several of the junior and middle school forms, which I greatly enjoyed.

One of the activities expected of English teachers in those days was to provide experience of drama by producing school plays. At Salford the tradition was to stage short, one-act plays with the junior children, especially the first form. I soon found myself roped into this though without any experience either of acting or production. Nevertheless all concerned threw ourselves into this activity with considerable energy and we had plenty of fun. One of my first productions was of a typical Lady Gregory play about the wearing of the green and the River Liffey. Even today I still retain a vivid memory of Albert Finney sitting on a barrel on the quay, giving me (as producer) a quizzical look. Finney was a charming and cooperative member of one of my first year forms; he had not been allotted the leading part. However it was probably his first dramatic performance. I have occasionally used this experience in talks on education to underline the fact that children's development is often unpredictable – and also that they may prove a great deal more talented than their teachers.

A note, 'Aspects of Schoolmastering', written after a year at

Salford, records some rewarding work on poetry by 13-year-olds, with the comment, 'teaching has its lighter moments'. A class of 14-year-olds 'really enjoy' Macbeth despite being rated exceptionally 'backward'. In this case, with the three witches going well with cracked voices 'flinging vipers' tongues and toads into the cauldron', I decided to take Macbeth myself. 'How now you ugly black and midnight hags', and I was well launched into the next great speech, the class avidly attentive and myself well worked up and going full steam, when the door opened to admit the mathematics teacher from the library next door. Half a dozen sixth formers were in there struggling manfully with a higher school certificate paper in (higher) mathematics. It was alright, he said, 'when the witches were on, but now . . .'. We migrated to the hall.

As form-master of first year pupils I found myself increasingly interested in the techniques used to allocate the 90 entrants to the three streams (A, B and C). One point familiar to all teachers, struck me forcibly. Extreme keenness, even enthusiasm, marked the great majority of entrants at eleven years of age. Alienation, lassitude, a general attitude of non-cooperation marked the lower streams three or four years later, especially the classes 3C and 4C. Anyone taking these classes on a Friday afternoon, or indeed at any time, could rely on the total sympathy of the entire staffroom. Although a select 20 per cent of their male age group within the grammar school, these children ended in classes which became ranked as pariahs, beyond hope of serious achievement.

What happened between the ages of 11 and 14 to create this situation, with all the loss of human potential it entailed? It occurred to me that the actual process by which children were categorised into graded classes might provide a clue, and I decided to investigate. At Salford the first year allocation of pupils into three separate streams rested on the results of the 11+ examination, set outside the school. This consisted of pencil and paper tests in 'Intelligence', Mathematics, English (the two latter being, in fact, very similar to 'Intelligence' Tests). The top thirty children were allocated to the A stream, the next to the B and the remaining third to the C stream. Since intelligence tests, it may be recalled, were then assumed to measure 'innate intellectual ability', this might seem, as it did then, a logical procedure.

I decided to run a mini-amateurish test of the system's efficiency, having learnt sufficient about statistical techniques to carry this through. At the end of the year *all* pupils in the three first forms (1A, 1B and 1C) sat the same examination in the main school subjects studied. If the initial allocation had been accurate, then, given the underlying assumption, the 1A pupils should generally have done best in the examination, 1C pupils worst, with 1B pupils betwixt and between.

I found the precise opposite. Overall 1C pupils did best in the first year examination, those who did least well were 1A, while 1B pupils were scattered randomly around. In short, in formal terms, the overall correlation between the first year examination results of these 90 pupils and their 11+ entry scores a year earlier was *negative*. This meant that, had the pupils with the lowest scores in the 11+ test been allocated to 1A, and those with the highest to 1C, categorisation of these pupils in terms of their achievement a year later would have been more accurate. At the time, the large claims advanced, and scarcely questioned, as to the predictive power of intelligence testing, dominated the mind – but my results prompted more sustained enquiry. After all, rather fundamental queries as to the educational implications and value of streaming arose, affecting arrangements throughout the school. In practice, at the end of each year pupils at the top of the B and C streams were moved up, while those at the bottom of the A and B streams were moved down. Moves in both directions appeared to affect the attitude and outlook of the pupils concerned. Those promoted into the top stream became increasingly conformist, passive in outlook – absorbers of facts; those relegated to the 'C' stream (sometimes highly 'intelligent' children – in terms of IQ – but 'troublemakers', or 'difficult') became increasingly alienated until, as indicated earlier, they became almost unteachable.

Almost by chance some further evidence questioning the validity of intelligence testing and selection came my way. In

Salford some children who had failed the 11+ and been relegated to secondary modern schools (or required to remain in their all-age elementary school) were given a second chance. At 13 some were allowed to sit a 'transfer' examination, once more comprising Intelligence, English and Mathematics. Each year three or four boys were successful and entered the grammar school as a result. These were then allocated to the B stream (3B) – since they had no Latin the A stream was barred to them. But what seemed to me striking was that, at the annual examinations, these 'transfer' boys emerged almost invariably at the top of the class.

Did this mean, given the opportunity, there were potentially hundreds of 11+ failures perfectly capable of doing well at grammar school? Why did only three or four boys get a transfer when those who passed did so well? Was the 13+ transfer examination relatively more difficult than that given at 11, and how could that be? I raised these issues informally with Stephen Wiseman – leading psychometrist at Manchester University and an expert on these affairs – when he visited the school, but he could produce no explanation. Although perhaps a minor point, the 13+ issue added to doubts about the validity of the selective process.

Seeking to learn more about all this, and as an addition to my professional qualifications, I now enrolled at the Manchester University School of Education to study for an M.Ed. (Master of Education). This involved lectures on two evenings a week for two years, submission of a dissertation and an examination. At the time Manchester had a national reputation as the leading centre of psychometric study in the country. The head of the education department, Professor R.A.C. Oliver, himself a psychometrist and research oriented, had established a reputation in this field when first appointed as a young man in the late 1930s, but the leading figures in the late 1940s were the psychologists Stephen Wiseman and Frank Warburton (both of whom had gained considerable experience of selective processes and techniques during war service in the army). The period from the late 1940s to the early 50s was a triumphal one for mental testing, when the theories evolved (and consequent practice) seemed to embody the most modern scientific procedures and thinking, properly applied to education. Every local authority in the country was now attempting to perfect selective procedures, once the Labour government adhered to the tripartite system which had been pointed to, though not enforced by, the 1944 Education Act. For a responsible authority it was necessary to devise reliable and defensible means and techniques to legitimise the practice. The 'Intelligence Test' seemed to provide precisely such a rationale, indeed acquired a virtual hegemony in educational thinking and practice.

The M.Ed. course embarked on in 1947 was directly focussed on the techniques and procedures of mental testing. This involved understanding complex statistical procedures such as those used in factor analysis, which underlay the whole business. Indeed my course might well be criticised for underplaying the study of education as such to insist so specifically on the statistical techniques appropriate to testing and also, to be fair, to the survey type of educational research popular at that time. However since I had already begun to develop my own critique of intelligence testing and was carrying through my own programme of reading and study in the area, attendance at an actual university-level course on the topic was, in a sense, an added bonus.

Indeed, after about four years teaching and some fairly concentrated reading, in an esoteric area of psychology, I formulated an initial challenge to the hegemony of mental testing which legitimated the highly selective system now emerging up and down the country. This was in response to an article in the Socialist press arguing that mental testing, particularly intelligence testing, was the most modern and scientifically legitimate approach to analysis of human mental development; and that its application to educational practice, in the form of streaming and selection, should be ever more widely propagated and realised.

By this time my own scepticism had grown to the point where I began to hold the opposite view – that human mental development depended primarily on the child's education and upbringing; that it was not finally determined by innate genetic endowment, according to the creed of the mental testing fraternity, not least its recently knighted leader, Cyril Burt. It was this view that I expressed in my article, one which had widespread support among progressive teachers at the time. Two other articles written at roughly the same time took the argument further. One put the *educational* case for the comprehensive secondary school in the light of a positive interpretation of children's educability, the other was a somewhat polemical critique of T.S. Eliot's thesis in *Notes Towards a Definition of Culture* (1948). Eliot argued that culture must remain a matter for the minority – that the idea of mass popular culture, a product of universal education, if realised, was and would be a disaster. Both a true education and a true culture must remain a matter for an elite. These were views widely propagated at the time, ideas to be contested openly if place was to be made for the positive educational thinking indispensable to meaningful intellectual and social advance.

This form of public engagement led to the recognition of the whole field of education in the context of its social and historical development. A Marxist approach led this way, but an immediate influence was Fred Clarke's seminal short book *Education and the Social Order*, published in 1940. Clarke introduced a stimulating sociological analysis to historical formation – a forerunner, in a sense, of a later school of socio-historians. To interpret educational development in its social relations and thereby reveal its social function, cast a new and rewarding light on the significance of educational change in relation to social change. By this route I came to a first venture into history – the preparation of a twelve session course for the Workers' Educational Association on 'Education and Society', dealing historically with educational change since the Reformation, but focussing specifically on the content of education rather than structural change. I still possess the fifty-plus pages of closely written notes for this course, the first two lectures of which were fully written out.

I remember well going one dusky October evening to an ex-elementary school in the centre of Manchester, where the local

WEA office directed me to find my class. No-one was there – neither from the WEA nor any students. Perhaps it was as well, the project was probably premature. But in later years both Joan and I turned to history, focussing respectively on the sixteenth and nineteenth centuries and, once at Leicester, on social history.

So our five years at Manchester and Salford drew to an end. I had long ago given up the idea of educational administration and was feeling that a university department of education was the place where the theory and practice of education could be followed up. In the spring of 1950 a place was advertised as Lecturer in Education, preparing graduates in English for teaching, in the then small university college of Leicester. One attraction was the recent appointment of the professor J.W. Tibble, who I had met at Exeter in the late 1930s when gathering material for the NUS book – a discussion that had greatly interested me. In 1950 most university education departments were dominated either by psychometrists as at Manchester and Birmingham, or members of what came to be known as 'Moberly's underworld'; that is educationists linked by a common aspiration to propagate Christian virtues as articulated in Walter Moberly's influential *The Crisis in the University* (1949). Tibble unusually adhered to neither school; his outlook was 'progressive' imbued with a sociological understanding.

The interview at Leicester was conducted by Frederick Attenborough, then in his last year as Principal of the College, the father of two sons who have since made great names for themselves. It was conducted, as I recall, in a gale of laughter. There were various professors there, no doubt, but Attenborough quickly established an easy rapport and the interview was really enjoyable. The job, however, was rightly offered to another candidate, much better qualified for it than myself, Geoffrey Bantock (who had both a first class degree in English from Cambridge, and many years' experience as lecturer in a well known training college at Leeds, plus publications – namely articles in a prestigious journal, *The Cambridge Review*). Nonetheless I was asked to stay behind, to be told by Tibble and the Registrar that the college had had several applications from ex-service students, funded on the Further Education and Training Scheme, seeking preparation to teach social studies in schools and colleges. Since I had a degree in economics, and had taught the subject and some social studies at Salford, they felt I was equipped for this job. Finance was evidently forthcoming. Offered it, I was glad to know that others had liked the interview, and to accept. My career as a university lecturer would begin at the ripe age of 35. My apprenticeship was over.

4

THE 1950S

THE EDUCATION DEPARTMENT, LEICESTER UNIVERSITY

Leicester University in 1997 has over 12,000 registered students, one of whom is my grand-daughter, studying psychology. There were only 600 at the University College in 1950 when I joined the staff, 80 of whom were in the education department. This was one of the largest departments; it had doubled in size since the previous year and the college, I found, took considerable pride in its work.

Up to the age of 35 my life had passed in five year stretches – at secondary school, university, in the army, and in apprenticeship to teaching at Manchester. Maybe at the back of my mind I expected another short stint, but as it turned out I remained for thirty years at a university which accorded generous treatment to its education department. This is by no means the general practice in the university world, which has traditionally looked down on the preparation of graduates for school teaching as an unsuitable adjunct to the academic life, and has been content to recruit its own teachers without any professional preparation whatsoever.

A number of institutions have, in the 1990s, been accorded full university status.This development has coincided with the continued increase in the number of students entering higher education; an expansion which seems to have taken place almost overnight. In contrast the immediate post-war years saw a planned and lengthy process of induction for the three small colleges, Leicester, Exeter and Hull, seeking to rise to university status. Before this students were prepared for London University degrees so that the colleges remained under external tutelage although recognised for grant by the University Grants Committee. But the Leicester education department was something of an exception. It had the power to devise its own syllabus leading to the award of a diploma (bringing recognised teacher status), subject only to ratification by the college authorities and the Ministry of Education.

Full use was made of this freedom by the first professor of education, J.W. Tibble, appointed in 1947. Formerly a member of the Exeter education department, he had realised some quite radical projects during the late 1930s and the war years, and continued in that vein. This was a second appointment to a full Chair; the first, in 1946, had been a professor of adult education. These two early appointments contributed to the high profile of the subject which was maintained and may have contributed to the award of university status in 1956. During my early years, the new department was rather particularly cared for and generously staffed. Perhaps the fact that Principal Attenborough had himself headed a leading teacher training college (Borough Road) had something to do with it. In any case the education department had got off to a good start.

The main function of the education department in the pre-university days was the training of graduates as teachers for both primary and secondary schools through a one year 'Diploma' course, or Postgraduate Certificate of Education (PGCE) as it was later called. Shortly there was established, in addition, an Institute of Education which provided a library, in-service courses, and other facilities for teachers and Training Colleges in the region; a product of the 1946 McNair Report on the Training of Teachers. The institute had its own staff and course structure and was funded to conduct research. Most universities established institutes of education at this time, usually appointing a Director who operated alongside the professor of education, heading the internal department. Unusually, at Leicester, the head of the education department was also appointed Director of the institute – and this was to have important effects later. In the 1950s teaching at the Institute was regarded as extra-curricular work.

Given the many ignorant attacks on practising teachers and their training in the 1990s, it is worthwhile describing the form of training we undertook. The department I joined was run on 'progressive' lines, reflecting Tibble's outlook and experience. It can best be described as 'student centred'. On the other hand there was a steady focus on learning, or gaining experience of, the actual task of teaching, in which it differed from most contemporary departments. Teacher education is still criticised as over-academic and insufficiently oriented towards preparation for the actual job of class teaching, but this was never the case at Leicester. Every student was part of a tutorial or 'method' group, covering a specific subject – history, English, maths, physics, chemistry, social studies and so on. During the initial autumn term, two mornings a week were devoted to this work; on one of which the entire group (then about eight students) were located at a specific school either teaching or as observers. Before the term began there had been a fortnight's 'preliminary course' also based at a chosen school, when both students and tutor taught classes and undertook a project relating to the school in its social setting. Like most other tutors I myself taught classes, observed by my students, both during this preliminary course and after.

During the Easter term, all students were based full-time at one (sometimes two) schools in the surrounding area for 'practice teaching' after a term's induction. Tutors visited their students throughout the term, on average in the early days about once a week. Students came into the department on Friday afternoons for general discussion with tutors and fellow students of experiences, problems and specific difficulties. In the summer term, arrangements reverted to something like the initial timetable, with 'method' groups working with tutors on two full mornings a week.

What I find quite striking, looking back on all this, is how far ahead Leicester of 1950 was by comparison with the London Institute, the norm only 13 years earlier – although, of course, wartime experience had intervened. This was also specifically due to generous financial treatment and an innovative professor, in Tibble, who knew his mind and exactly what he wanted to do. Certainly a carefully planned stress on the business of professional training was a key feature of the Leicester course – the means whereby teachers were effectively *qualified* as professionals.

The organisation of students into 'method groups' was only one aspect of a course conceived by Tibble as an induction into the educational field at large. This included allowing the students time for reflection and reading, for pursuit of particular interests; and gave staff scope to develop their own interests outside the teaching of a specialist subject. There was, in addition, a general course on education, originally conducted in lecture form by the two professors. As a lecturer or seminar leader Tibble had a Socratic style which I much admired but could never emulate. There were long silences; questions were raised, touched on, and left gently hanging in the air. But the role was abandoned when he became fully involved in the politics of teacher education at national level and was often away. It was then taken over by junior staff, notably Robin Pedley, with whom I was to work jointly promoting comprehensive education; otherwise Geoffrey Bantock whose approach by comparison was highly traditional, or me. The rather diverse views may well have stimulated students to think for themselves.

Optional seminar or discussion group courses, offered by all members of the staff, supplemented the general courses. This enabled me to offer courses in the history of education (which rapidly became a main field of interest), and, in due course, on comprehensive education, permitting more detailed study by students with a special interest in this area. In the early evenings, various optional 'activities'were set up by staff members with a special interest or expertise, or others invited to promote music, drama, dance. Bob Wight, Director of Physical Education for the university – but also a member of our staff (and a close friend) – offered orienteering and other outdoor or sporting activities during the week. When, therefore, I say the course was 'student centred', this was because in taking up options each student constructed a timetable corresponding to interests and predilections. Staff also had scope, or choice, in terms of the topic or activity offered. In theory, then, everybody should have been fully involved, valued and motivated. If this was not always the case there was, I would say, effective interaction between students and staff.

A crucial concomitant of such an approach was the absence of a final examination. Assessment was made by 'coursework'; that is, assessed essays on agreed subjects each term with a minor thesis or 'dissertation' at the close of the course. But assessment of practical teaching was the traditional pattern by staff assisted by external examiners.

I have mentioned earlier Helen Wodehouse's achievement as Professor of Education at Bristol in the 1930s: the elimination of a final examination as inappropriate for graduate students who, by definition, had already passed finals in specialist subjects. But this had been the only department to achieve this breakthrough by agreement with the Bristol senate. Determined that his department would take this road, Tibble persuaded the Leicester senate to agree it. The London Institute's final examination had seemed to me, as a student, farcical. I have no doubt that the system of 'continuous assessment', espoused at Leicester, contributed markedly to the success of the department. Very gradually, most (if not all) universities fell into line including, in the early 1970s, belatedly enough, the London Institute of Education itself.

My own priority at Leicester was to prepare an effective course for students preparing to teach social studies in secondary schools (or, in some cases, technical colleges). Most of these students had recently completed military service; this meant an older, more widely experienced, intake than the normal set of 21 year-old graduates. Many were motivated by the progressive post-war outlook so characteristic of young people then, and as anxious to get into the 'real world' as I had been. So this was a very rewarding group for a new lecturer taking a relatively new kind of course to induct into the profession; students who could be relied upon to be critical and articulate in seminars and discussions, who generally had a responsible attitude to work, which brought an active interest in the broader educational issues beyond teaching.

To prepare a course for these students was, therefore, not too difficult; focused, as it had to be, on problems of teaching and learning in social studies. Alongside the social studies seminars was a 'topic' course on the history of education. I attempted to make this both relevant and stimulating, so it was useful to have to hand studies begun at Manchester, which bore on the main factors determining educational development from the late eighteenth century.

HISTORY OF EDUCATION

The university provided a new vantage point for study and analysis of the public system of education. By 1951 there was also a new government; the Labour administration had resigned, then lost the subsequent election – though polling its highest ever vote – which registered continuing support for reforms. By contrast Florence Horsbrugh, the Conservative Minister of Education, was not even accorded a seat in the Cabinet. But she soon ranked as so enthusiastic an economiser that the Prime Minister, Winston Churchill, had to curb her initiatives. She also strongly opposed comprehensive education, though popular pressure for change was growing. There had been nothing much to be said for Labour ministers in this connection, but Conservative policy was backward-looking generally. This propelled me into action on two fronts: in relation on the one hand to earlier enquiries into testing, selection, the Intelligence Quotient, and on the other the history of education.

It is difficult to reconstruct the extraordinary hegemony that the theory and practice of intelligence testing came to exercise over the field of education. The theory holding sway in the 1950s derived primarily from Cyril Burt: as he had put the matter back in the early 1930s 'Intelligence' ('g') was the dominant 'factor of the mind' – inborn, genetically determined, it was impervious to any change whether by education or any other life experiences. 'Fortunately', Burt complacently affirmed in a popular radio series, Intelligence 'can be measured with accuracy and ease'. As every child was born with a fixed level of intelligence, each must be provided with the education 'for which he seems to have been marked out'.

The theory neatly legitimated a fractured and divisive education system which had been formed historically in response to the policies of parties in government through decades. You could not tell a one-time teacher of Abbott Street all-age elementary school children that a standard IQ test would fairly assess the children's human capacity; while relatively superficial observations at Salford Grammar School seriously questioned the 11-plus selection process.

History had its own explanations of the origins and practice of selection. Once cut off altogether from secondary schooling, the elementary school had made its way up into 'Higher Grade Schools' which flourished – but were then ruled out in favour of the narrowest of routes, for a small percentage of children, into 'grammar' schools. Even the 1944 Act with its provision for secondary education for all, unavoidable in wartime, did not secure this, leaving the way open for a tripartite secondary system preserving in first place the selective grammar school. Labour had adhered to this structure immediately after the war. The Conservatives, once again in power after 1951, continued to curb opportunities for the majority – cutting back resources so that the nation's children too often studied in broken down, insanitary buildings; in over-large classes, without necessary equipment.

That much had been underlined by study of the history of education – a subject not followed in most departments of history, and only built up on its own account since the turn of the century; in the main because of the extension of teacher-training colleges (and university education departments). I was fortunate that my position at Leicester – teaching a social science method group – bordered on this area. Then there was the additional opportunity of giving twelve one-and-a-half hour sessions, weekly, in the autumn term, in the history of education topic group. From this point I began to delve more deeply into the history of education.

I soon found myself in a fascinating area of study, at the time relatively untilled. The received 'textbook' version of the provision of education for the working class described it as the outcome of a benevolent philanthropic movement, which, from the early nineteenth century, was motivated to act. The elementary schools established using the newly developed monitorial system were administered by 'voluntary bodies' – the British and Foreign School Society (on the whole non-conformist), and the Church of England, working through the National Society. These sought, between 1820-40, to widen access to education by building schools throughout the country. Nothing was said or, it appears, even known by the authors of texts about indigenous, even clamorous, efforts by working people to provide education themselves, nor of their sometimes heroic efforts at self-education. As my investigations continued, it seemed increasingly evident that provision of schooling *for* the working people during these years could best be interpreted as a direct reaction to this drive on the part of ordinary people to educate themselves. It could also be seen as a response to the radicalisation of working people, especially in the industrial north; in Lancashire and Yorkshire where there was a political transformation during the forty years between 1790 and 1830.

Not myself a historian I sought help from an old Cambridge friend, James Klugmann, fellow Communist and bibliophile, who shared a house in north London with Maurice Cornforth. Cornforth was at this time director of the publishing firm Lawrence and Wishart, and married to Klugmann's sister, Kitty. The second floor, staircase included, belonged to James and was replete with books, journals, historical prints and caricatures, ephemera of all kinds, (coins, medals, china) – especially if they had any bearing on the Labour movement. Every kind of book, popular and rare, filled the shelves, covered the bedroom (except the bed), piled on the stairs, and silted up both floor and walls in his 'sitting room' – leaving a space no more than four feet square accomodating a small wooden table and chair. His collection was already fantastic by the 1950s when I went there to work on material beyond the conception of the University College's library. Over the next decades, though once ravaged by fire, the collection expanded greatly until the owner's death in 1977. The best of the collection now rests at the Marx House Library in Clerkenwell and the Labour History Museum at Manchester.

James Klugmann introduced me to the wealth of literature – mainly pamphlets and journals – thrown up by the independent working-class and radical movement; from the Corresponding Societies of the 1790s, through the Hampden Clubs, Secular Sunday Schools, and Political Protestants to the flowering of Chartism from the late 1830s. Journals like the *Black Dwarf*, packed with relevant matter, stood side by side on his library shelves with Cobbett's *Register* and Carlile's *Republican*. There were also copies of larger works, dealing directly with education – such as Carlile's *Address to Men of Science* (1821), the cooperator William Thompson's *Inquiry into the Distribution of Wealth* (1824), Lovett's *Chartism* (1841) – alongside Thomas Hodgkin's *Labour Defended against the Claims of Capital* (1825), John Gray's *Lecture on Human Happiness* (1825). All this was an absolute eye-opener. There had been no reference to this entire movement in the textbook histories I had consulted. Some historians had begun to plumb this area; but not in terms of its educational impact and significance. One thing this study brought home very clearly. A proper history of popular education must extend over an area far wider than established schooling, to cover a population often educating itself, reading, talking, discussing. This had little or nothing to do with schools then in existence. It was another world; but, by implication, one demanding a response from authority.

My first serious attempt at analysis developed gradually, through a combination of study and research, teaching the topic to students in lectures (always a stimulus) and searching for an explanatory pattern which made sense of the enormous amount of material available. It became apparent that initiatives of the early Labour or Radical movement had generated a response; the one formulated by the nascent bourgeoisie of that period I delineate as the Radical Theory of Universal Enlightenment. Jeremy Bentham, James Mill and their colleagues pressed the case for universal education, under strict control, as a crucial step towards a common front with the 'labouring poor' in the fight to oust aristocracy and landed interest from control. Hence 'the democratic model' they advanced – by way of universal franchise, plus education, power would be transferred through a reformed Parliament, to the bourgeoisie. In the event that alliance was broken by the exclusionary nature of the 1832 Reform Act. Thereafter the industrial and landed interests coincided politically and socially, and, through the establishment of the 'public schools' as a system, also educationally. The state became the prime mover in an almost total reconstruction of educational provision in the two decades 1850-70. And so, by the end of the nineteenth century, the hierarchical structure which marks the English system was established. To all intents and purposes this had been achieved by 1870, the Education Act of that year setting the seal on the whole construction (that is why this first volume ends with the passage of that Act).

The first chapter of *Studies In The History Of Education 1780-1870*, 'Forerunners of Educational Reform', dealt with the famous Lunar Society of the 1780s and the accompanying Literary and Philosophical Societies of Manchester and elsewhere. Essentially the English (and Scottish) expression of the Enlightenment, these groups expressed faith in the power of education to further human perfectibility. I discovered that four of the fourteen members of the Lunar Society (of Birmingham) wrote major works on education – Priestley, Edgeworth, Day, Darwin. Humanist and essentially optimistic in their outlook they were deeply concerned, as all educationists should be, with learning and teaching. The people this group represented – industrialists, scientists and professional men – were concerned with moral and social, as well as intellectual development. But as time went on the broad humanist perspective narrowed to the level of utilitarianism – the outlook elaborated in Bentham's

Chrestomathia – and the more directly political objectives of James Mill.

How and why this transition took place still seems to me to require interpretation. My own conclusion was that the Lunar Society ideals were espoused and developed by radical and working-class leaders in the 1830s and 40s, and may be traced anew in the work of William Morris. I was fascinated by all these people, even such minor characters as Mary Ann Schimmelpenninck. The epitaph on the Lunar Society, written in 1809 by Francis Horner, after a visit to its Birmingham centre Soho, still moves me. It seems as relevant to our times as it was almost two hundred years ago.

> The remnants of the Lunar Society, and the fresh remembrance in others, of the remarkable men who composed it, are very interesting; the impression which they made is not yet worn out, but shows itself, to the second and third generations, in a spirit of scientific curiosity and free enquiry, which even yet makes some stand against the combined forces of Methodism, Toryism, and the love of gain.

My initial move into the history of education was a decade, at least, in preparation (amongst much other work, of course!) The need to present a coherent set of lectures to our postgraduate students helped materially, and during the years the history of education was upgraded to a 'core course' for all students. I planned originally a book to cover the years up to the crucial 1902 Education Act, indeed to 1914. But as material accumulated, the complexity of changing circumstances in the nineteenth century engaged extended attention and I decided to make the break at, or around, 1870.

There was more general interest in the history of education in the late 1950s than today, as evidenced by several sympathic reviews of *Studies in the History of Education 1780-1870* – interesting to look back on in 1997. Raymond Williams was welcoming, if muted, finding me 'a frank and intelligent partisan, both in politics and in education', but the book was 'scholarly, full of interesting detail, very well illustrated, and clear and easy to read' (*Guardian*, 14.4.1960). Margaret Cole found three great merits. It was 'very readable', unusual in books on the subject, 'quotes largely from original sources', and brought together the story of 'all kinds of education during the period – for the rich, the middle classes and the poor' (*Tribune* 15.4.1960). Fellow historians of education were friendly – A.V. Judges, H.C. Barnard, by then the doyen in this field, W.H.G. Armytage, the energetic and ebullient Professor of Education at Sheffield. H.C. Dent, product of an elementary school, was a knowledgeable commentator (*Schoolmaster* 10.6.1960), and the book was noticed in the Labour movement press generally. The *Times Educational Supplement* took objection to my interpretation of the role of the state in mid-century but conceded that the author had 'studied his sources with meticulous care' and become thoroughly familiar with the period to produce a well arranged, 'lucidly written' book bearing 'the impress of a vigorous and well-stored mind'. For the Welsh historian, Gwyn A. Williams, this was 'a full and balanced study in the sophisticated Marxist mode'.

There was reason to be pleased with all this. So much for a first foray into recording and interpreting the history of education in this country.

THE CRITIQUE OF INTELLIGENCE TESTING

To follow the history of educational ideas and institutions into the twentieth century, as I had begun to do, was to familiarise myself with the story of the rise of mental measurement, and in particular 'Intelligence Testing'. Following World War Two, Hadow reorganisation was pressed ahead with some energy, bringing with it new forms of inner school organisation, particularly the precise grading and streaming of pupils in the new primary schools in preparation for 11 plus selection. But the idea of the 'multilateral' school, increasingly referred to as 'comprehensive', was still there, having been espoused as official policy by both the Labour and Communist parties, and supported by many non-political educationists. With a Conservative government in power, the tripartite system of technical, secondary modern and grammar schools was firmly endorsed. The pressure for change also strengthened. It seemed to many that the mortar holding together the fractured and divisive education system lay in the theory and practice of intelligence testing, which dominated, but above all, legitimated school selection at eleven and inner school differentiation from the age of seven and sometimes five.

There was a need to de-mystify what seemed to many an arcane and secret 'science'. To do so meant a head-on critique of current claims made for intelligence testing in its direct application to education. I believed that such a critique should be understandable to parents and all interested in the nation's schools. It was this that I attempted fairly soon after my arrival at Leicester.

My concerns centred on the actual techniques used to construct tests: the underlying assumptions that were then adopted as 'the truth' by psychologists and others. A crucial factor for believers in I.Q. testing was that 'Intelligence' was, and always must be, 'normally distributed'; others related to the suitability of techniques governing validation and standardisation. It was argued that a class element enters into the practice of intelligence testing at almost every stage: firstly, and most importantly, in the choice and character of the questions; secondly, in the method of compiling test questions and validating the test as a whole; finally, in the process of standardisation. These processes together serve to militate against the success of the more culturally deprived children. The fact that surveys showing the average Intelligence Quotient of the more advantaged social classes is greater than that of the working class was sometimes cited as proof of a justly established social order is the best possible confirmation that a kind of confidence trick has been mounted.

I have been citing, in part, from the little book that emerged in 1953, *Intelligence Testing and the Comprehensive School*. It also discussed the validity of secondary school selection in some detail, highlighting the success of 11 plus rejects who had been offered other opportunities. In sum it could be argued that mental testing had failed. As there could clearly be no return to discredited procedures of selection, what had turned into a fruitless and sterile search for a perfect selection technique should be abandoned. The educational solution was apparent: to close down the divided system and engender a real secondary education for all, thereby opening opportunities for systematic and purposeful teaching of all children alike. Once in place the comprehensive school would allow for a transformation of primary as well as secondary schools.

One way or another this short book made some mark. A preface by a grammar school head and wartime president of the NUT recommended it as likely to make a major impact. More letters came in to me personally from unknown writers, as well as colleagues, than I have had from any other publication. On this occasion the *Times Educational Supplement* characterised the book as 'a formidable indictment of the theory and practice of intelligence testing' concluding that 'the case stands up'; the arguments advanced 'should draw a reply from the defence', couched in language 'as comprehensible as that of the prosecution' (15.1.1954). In the *New Statesman* (27.3.54) John Garrett, headmaster of Bristol Grammar School, and no proponent of comprehensive education, also decided that the case 'deserves respect and demands an answer'. Writing in the *New Era*, organ of the New Education Fellowship, James Hemming, a well-known psychologist, found the book showed 'with devastating force that what is left of the theory of tripartism is a mass of unreality, injustice, distortion and pretence'.

There was, naturally enough, a very different reaction from psychometrists, whose primary concern was mental measurement. The consultant to the National Foundation of Educational Research, then a powerhouse of psychometry – especially test construction and marketing, to serve local authorities – was Dr Watts. He condemned my arguments as misleading, remarked that it was a pity educational discussion should be brought down 'to the tub-thumping level of backbench party politics'; the book's main thesis was 'too silly to merit rational discussion, except perhaps in the pages of a journal devoted to psychotherapy' (*Journal of Education*, April 1954). My Manchester University M.Ed. tutor, Stephen Wiseman, writing for the *Labour Teacher* (organ of the National Association of Labour Teachers) found a 'grave and fundamental error' which 'makes the whole content of the book suspect and does the Communist case more harm than good'; though, when challenged in the journal, he did not substantiate the point. It was a pity, he concluded somewhat inconsequently, 'the book does the job so badly'.

A year later there was an expert evaluation of techniques used in mental testing and the educational implications of selection. *The Appraisal of Intelligence*, by Alice Heim, was widely reviewed in the educational and psychological press, and Cyril Burt's biographer was later to say that the two analyses, professional and amateur, opened a first wave of criticism which drove Cyril Burt on to the road of deceit.[1] 'His two twin articles of 1955 and 1966 were his rejoinders as he himself makes clear ... motivated by a determination to get the better of his critics'. It was data presented in these articles that were later exposed as fraudulent. 'They were written in haste and anger'.

As concern about the use of intelligence testing for selective purposes increased among psychologists new voices were heard. P.E.Vernon, Professor of Educational Psychology at the University of London Institute of Education, took the lead. He was genuinely troubled and anxious to find a way through the difficulties, gradually distancing himself from the classic, hard-line theory of intelligence formulated by Burt. He had also reviewed my contribution in the *British Journal of Psychology* (June 1954) giving me credit for studying the technicalities of the subject 'more thoroughly than most propagandists ... and his distortions are remarkably few'. 'A serious case' resulted which 'deserves a serious answer'. In any case, Vernon declared, the time was ripe 'for psychologists to get together and attempt to decide how far their instruments are doing harm, and how they could be better employed'.

The outcome was a committee of 14, manned by professors of education and leading psychometrists (Stephen Wiseman included) under the chairmanship of Vernon. Three years on, in 1957, came their report, *Secondary School Selection*. The main conclusions countered the inordinate claims advanced for several decades, in effect ending the hegemony of mental testing. After a close examination of relevant issues the report favoured the abolition of streaming in junior schools (as this exacerbated individual differences) and the introduction of comprehensive education, at least for the early years. 'Any policy involving immediate irreversible segregation at 11 years or earlier is psychologically unsound', it was stated. Consequently 'insofar as public opinion allows – the common or comprehensive school would be preferable at least to the age of 13' (pp 43-4, 53). By destroying the ideological foundations of the tripartite system this report marked a crucial turning point in the swing to comprehensive secondary education.

The official critique specifically took up the main theoretical issues raised in my little book. Is 'Intelligence' an innate quality of the mind? By what objective criteria could it be measured? What evidence is there that intelligence normally remains stable for individual children? What unexamined assumptions are embodied in the choice of questions (items) in tests? How valid are the statistical techniques used to construct tests and interpret their results? How far are these items class conditioned? But although *Secondary School Selection* expressed an intention 'to set out the arguments for and the weaknesses of intelligence tests rationally and impartially' (p88) this proved difficult to live up to. The report consistently imputes bias to the more radical critics, labelled 'left wing', while claiming to propound 'common-sense'. However, it could do no other than distance psychologists from a hitherto implicit faith in the predictive power of test results, and this meant formulating a more flexible theory of 'Intelligence'. This in turn allowed for criticism of early determination of a child's future through rigid streaming and selection, and marked a new phase in conceptualising 'ability'.

In 1970, when concern about testing once more rose to new heights, my book was reprinted, with later essays on psychology and education, to sell another 4000 copies. But it was the 1953 edition that counted and led on to further enquiry and travel. A leading Russian neuropsychologist, A.R. Luria – though not so known in England – arranged for this book to be published in Moscow, himself taking on the role of editor. I had gradually learned something about the work of the leading psychologists in the Soviet Union whose research in education penetrated in a new way into the learning process in young children; research directly related to improving methods of teaching in the schools. Despite the Cold War the Soviet Union had invested heavily in education; their novel approaches to teaching and learning called for recognition. The influential work of Lev Vygotski, derived directly from the revolutionary years of the 1920s, overtly rejected the fatalistic theories dominant in England. The overriding belief was in human potential, in educability. Luria had been a close colleague of Vygotski (who died young) but by then had a high reputation in the West for an early book of his own. Luria now saw to it that my *Intelligence Testing and the Comprehensive School* appeared in Russia in 1958. So began a long partnership and close friendship. It was not to be long before the compliment was returned.

It all began in 1955 with an invitation from the Academy of Educational Sciences of the USSR, a body which comprised leading academics and scholars in both education and psychology, and controlled all the leading research institutes. The invitation was a general one, to British educationists for a month's visit to the USSR under the academy's aegis. There had been something of a thaw in international relations after Krushchev became General Secretary of the Communist Party, but the Soviet Union remained markedly unpopular and only two educationists of any standing elected to accept – Lady Simon of Wythenshawe, my mother, then over 70 (who I was glad to accompany), and the principal of the Swansea Teacher Training College. A fourth member of the select party was a

London comprehensive school teacher who had taught in Moscow before the war, Deana Levin. Regardless of our relative lack of importance the leading members of the academy readily put themselves out to meet our requests and demands.

It soon became abundantly clear, during visits to schools and research institutes, that the most serious research in the Soviet Union lay in the field of the psychology of learning, and the best use I personally could make of a month's visit was to learn as much about this as possible. Luria worked at what was then called the Institute of Defectology, where research was conducted into what we now call 'learning difficulties', a change of nomenclature testifying to alteration of viewpoints. During early visits here, as to the Institute of Psychology, I was struck by the success of psychologists concentrating on learning activity, a practice largely ignored in England.

Mental testing produced (as it were) a snapshot of human potential by use of tests, supposedly pinpointing genetic make-up determining cognitive ability, this being seen as an hereditary endowment. Soviet psychologists, however, were interested in abilities resulting from processes of historical formation. No-one was born with a given ability, it was held, though perhaps with a pre-disposition towards certain activities. Abilities are formed in the process of the child's education and life experiences. So education is all important of an order to maximise the formation of abilities.

Nor was this all. There was an emphasis in psychological and educational research on the crucial role of language in mental development, a finding originating with Vygotski and underlined by current projects, not least those of Luria. Within the Institute of Defectology there were extraordinary advances in the education of those customarily labelled 'ineducable', particularly those with multiple defects: the blind, deaf and dumb. One of the most moving experiences was a talk with a member of staff who, from childhood, had suffered in this way but had been educated at the institute. The recent outcome had been two books in which she had expressed and analysed her experience, *How I Perceive the World* and *How I Conceive the World*.

Several leading psychologists besides Luria had been co-workers with Lev Vygotski, notably Leontiev and Zaphorozets whose approach to the study of mental development and learning remained in the tradition – one that, in the 1990s, has been adopted with enthusiasm in the United States and taken up here. But in the 1950s it was a question of introducing these ideas;we had discussions about producing a symposium comprising key articles covering the main areas of research. The idea was to cover what we call educational psychology with papers on child development, speech and thought, and, specifically, psychology of the formation of mental abilities, the sphere of Leontiev and Galperin. Clearly the research of Soviet colleagues could testify to the viability of a fresh understanding of teaching and learning, and indeed to an optimistic view of human development, stressing the educability of the normal child – the crying need if the road was to be opened to an effective form of schooling at home.

The project quickly gained energetic cooperation from A.A. Smirnov, the much respected Director of the Institute of Psychology, and Luria immediately offered a special chapter on psycho-pathological research in the USSR. Otherwise the contents of the book were worked out in Moscow, and Professor Smirnov, after a general discussion with colleagues, sent 30 papers. Of these twenty were chosen for translation and submission to a publisher. Routledge and Kegan Paul published then regular contributions to an 'International Library of Sociology and Social Reconstruction' under the editorship of W.J.H. (Sebastian) Sprott, Professor of Psychology at Nottingham. He was very ready to take on the symposium and remained warmly encouraging throughout publication of this particular book and, as it turned out, its successor. A massive translation job was undertaken, by four well qualified friends, and the book appeared in 1957 – only two years after the Moscow visit. Also published in the United States by Stanford University Press, it was chosen as 'Book of the Month' by Basic Books. This first publication in English of Soviet psychological research was well received in England but more especially in the United States.

In the autumn of this same year Alexander Luria paid his first visit to England, invited by the University of London, where he lectured to large audiences on his special field – the diagnosis and education of handicapped children. He arrived on the same day as the successful launch of the first Soviet sputnik, an event which shook the world. Luria also came to Leicester and stayed with us, lecturing at the Midlands branch of the British Psychological Society. 'I am like the satellite', Alex told the local reporter, with a world circling motion of his hand, 'I am here for too short a time'. The lecture, of course, was a great success – Luria could deliver an English speech of one and a half hours without a note, and without hesitation. The only thing that held him up was my inability to insert quickly and efficiently the clumsy, old-fashioned slides he had brought with him into a creaking machine.

As my wife Joan vividly recalls, Luria came into the sitting room the next morning with a small book in his hand. 'I wonder', he said a little hesitantly, handing it over, 'whether it would be possible to translate this little book?' In the event it was feasible; Joan took on the job with the help of an Estonian living in Leicester. *Speech and the Development of Mental Processes in the Child* (1959) is now famous among psychologists and educators all over the world. It was the first book that brought to the sphere of education, in popular and intelligible form, the Vygotskian view on the crucial role of language in mental development.

The experimental research recorded, on identical twins, had been undertaken in the 1930s in Moscow but only considered for publication in the USSR in 1956. This time Staples Press took it on, and published it in 1959 with a foreword by the Professor of Experimental Psychology at Cambridge, Oliver Zangwill, an old friend from the 1930s who also became a close friend of Luria's. The 'little book' had been launched and was well received in the specialist press, but initially sales were not so encouraging.

The subsequent publishing history has been extraordinary. After selling a few hundred copies each year – it had sold about 1000 in the early 1960s – sales suddenly took off, until in 1970 a Penguin reprint gained a very wide distribution and requests to publish translations of the *English* edition came from Denmark, West Germany, Sweden and France. This symbolised a willingness on the part of these countries to consider previously 'alien' concepts. The question of another symposium was also on the agenda. While *Psychology in the Soviet Union* had aroused interest among professional psychologists (and been widely reviewed), it had little immediate impact on the circle still convinced by the merits of mental testing. Meanwhile there was scope to turn from psychology to education.

THE COMPREHENSIVE SCHOOL: FOR NEW TRENDS IN EDUCATION

My main work, apart from the time for research a university job allowed, remained focused on the preparation of secondary school teachers. It involved direct experience of many schools, their achievements and problems, much as my own training had done. The main problem constantly to the fore here, though, in educational rather than psychological terms, was that of school organisation at the secondary level. The 1944 Act had been engineered to impose a tripartite system involving the development of three types of secondary school. But by the early 1950s it was evident that secondary technical schools had not seriously taken off; the grammar school was now increasingly perceived as problematic while the new secondary modern schools never found their way.

The alternative was, of course, the multilateral or comprehensive school catering for all from the age of eleven. At the time, the dominant concept here was the huge school, planned by the London County Council (a plan only now beginning to be implemented). The Ministry of Education itself insisted that such schools should include a minimum of 1600 pupils, in order to provide sufficient intake of high IQ children to make up an adequate 'sixth form'. It became clear that it was necessary to tackle this issue at the organisational level, and to show that such large schools, whose rationale depended on IQ theory, were unnecessary and that alternative, more practical forms of the common school could more easily be established. In this the lead nationally was taken by Robin Pedley, a colleague at Leicester.

There had been discussion of comprehensive education in the 1940s and early 1950s but little had been written on the topic. One exception was a book written by my mother, Shena Simon, who drew on experience gained in administration and in travel. A visit to the United States during the war had proved deeply influential, supplemented by one to Scotland (with Joan in 1947) to see several what were then called 'omnibus schools'. Drawing on these experiences, *Three Schools or One?* (No. 1 in a series 'Questions of the Day' published by Muller), presented a rational and carefully thought out, in no sense ideological, case for the comprehensive school. In effect 'the comprehensive high school could become . . . the common secondary school for the people. It could substitute new values for those which survive from a previous age, which we now realise to be inconsistent with democracy'. For the next twenty or more years, until her death at eighty-eight in 1972, Shena Simon consistently encouraged every step taken in this direction.

Taking a hint from this I turned my attention to accumulating information about common (multilateral, comprehensive) schools in England; or making a case for *The Common Secondary School*, as my contribution was to be headed. The aim was to pool the experience of the few comprehensive schools belatedly surfacing; this coincided with the interests of Robin Pedley. So it was that, in the spring of 1954, we made plans to visit together every functioning comprehensive school in England and Wales. It was not so difficult a task as might now be imagined, there were no more than thirteen. Of these, eight were on Anglesey and the Isle of Man, the rest were scattered two in Middlesex, one apiece in Westmorland and the West Riding and one at Walsall. Somewhat other were those established, as an earnest of future development, by the London County Council; 'interim' comprehensive schools (as it were, half way there) from which it was hoped to gain experience in running large schools. Both Robin and I had friends among the teachers and heads of

London schools, and these were also visited.

We were impressed – perhaps most by the entire local 'system' developed in Anglesey where, in 1953, the 11 plus had just been abolished. Two of their schools were new, and purpose-built, at Llangefni and Amlwych; a third, at Holyhead,was formed by the merger of a grammar and adjacent secondary modern school. All seemed to be operating well and morale was high. Standing with Trevor Lovett, head of Holyhead, as pupils of both sexes trooped into the canteen for lunch, we were challenged to tell the difference between ex-grammar and secondary modern pupils. Of course it was impossible. The challenge was to the point given the tendency to regard the two sets of pupils as of different species.

Unfortunately I was unable to accompany Robin to the Isle of Man where there was also a complete system of comprehensive schools – again four to serve the island as a whole. Here he was particularly impressed by Castle Rushen School, a small comprehensive of four hundred and fifty pupils, in clear contrast to the large London schools. William Cretney was to become the first head of a comprehensive school to be knighted, so conferring traditional respectability on the new movement. Castle Rushen served a community function very effectively, and like the even smaller Windermere School of about two hundred, demonstrated that the small comprehensive could be viable.

Robin Pedley used very effectively his accumulated data to buttress the case for a 'two-tier' comprehensive system with a break at sixteen. There were small, uneconomic sixth-forms in the schools we visited and he was convinced that the solution was viable; it not only allowed for smaller schools than the 11-18 variant, but ensured a more mature treatment of sixteen-year-olds than in normal schools. The idea aroused much interest and three articles by Pedley were reprinted (by Councils and Education Press) in 1954 with extended comments by leaders of opinion (Harold Dent, Eric James, Harold Sherman) and interested local administrators. This was a breakthrough in putting comprehensive schools on the map as a practical proposition, particularly as it allowed, if necessary, for the use of existing buildings. Local authority officers, among them Leicestershire's CEO Stewart Mason, were coming under increasingly heavy pressure, not least from disgruntled parents whose children had failed the 11 plus and been automatically relegated to secondary modern schools which could offer few perspectives. Here was a new body of support for an alternative secondary school.

My contribution, *The Common Secondary School,* appeared in May 1955. After dealing with the problems emerging in selection and recalling criticism of tests made earlier, the book argued the case for the single secondary school with a common curriculum; one covering the main areas of knowledge and skills and culminating at sixteen with a single examination designed to mark the end of the first stage of secondary education. A chapter on practical policy suggested stages whereby a local comprehensive 'system', catering for a single city and utilising existing buildings, might be established. At this time the associations of grammar school teachers were conducting a desperate, last-ditch, campaign against comprehensive education, with the support of the Conservative government. The dismissive headings of some reviews reflect the atmosphere: 'Common Equality' (*Education*), 'Omnium Gathorum' (*Times Educational Supplement*), 'Too Simple' (*Times Literary Supplement*). But if most reviewers wished to distance themselves from the conclusions of the book, it was more welcome in the educational and labour movement press including, interestingly, several trade union journals.

The breadth of support was a feature of the gathering movement towards comprehensive education in the late 1950s. Pedley, who engaged in it with considerable energy, was a Labour party supporter but not politically inclined; there were very varied political views among the many heads and teachers of the newly formed comprehensive schools in London, Coventry and elsewhere. It was time for teachers to speak for themselves. Those teaching both in secondary modern and comprehensive-type schools could best convey new developments and, most important, point the way towards a common curriculum. I began by commissioning a number of heads and teachers for articles covering unstreaming in the junior school, new perspectives in secondary modern schools (where there were attempts to burst through restrictive conditions), and early experience in proto-comprehensive schools whatever they were called ('interim', 'bilateral' and comprehensive). The plan was a book on these topics, which would include some articles by teachers in these latter schools on the development of a common syllabus for all pupils in such schools: in English, science, mathematics, modern languages and history (by George Rudé, in due course a distinguished historian).

New Trends in English Education materialised early in 1957 with the sympathetic and enthusiastic assistance of publishers MacGibbon and Kee. The leading executive who handled it, Poynter Davis, was himself actively engaged in the ultimately successful movement to establish comprehensive schooling in the 'new town' of Crawley. The book testified to the possibility of a broad alliance between teachers and others across political spectra to achieve an overdue transformation of the educational system.

Meanwhile Pedley had published the influential and widely reviewed *Comprehensive Education, a New Approach* (Gollancz 1956). What was 'new' here was his advocacy of the 'county college' system, spelt out in some detail, developing the conception of county colleges serving the educational and recreational needs of a neighbourhood or community.

So Leicester, now a full university, was becoming rather well known as a centre for new thinking about education. The education department was well able to contend with a variety of convictions as Geoffrey Bantock was also gaining prominence as a scholarly upholder of traditional and grammar school values.

New Trends emerged at just about the right time, and was well received. It put junior school unstreaming on the map for perhaps the first time. An article by George Freeland on experience in his Leicester school, was written up in *News Chronicle*, the now defunct Liberal daily. Several local newspapers highlighted the book while in *Tribune* Jennie Lee gave it whole-hearted support, as did Michael Stewart, a future

Secretary of State for Education and Science, in the *New Statesman*. The professional press was equally friendly.

While contributing markedly to discussion among teachers about aspects of organising comprehensive schools, the book was, I think, in making the case for a common curriculum for all pupils, some thirty years ahead of its time. It also offered a more generous perspective than the National Curriculum following on the 1988 Education Act.

According to official statistics the 13 schools of the comprehensive sector visited by Pedley and me in 1954 grew to 31 in 1956 and to 43 in 1957; the next year the number doubled to 86, though these schools educated less than 1 per cent of pupils in maintained secondary schools. Although this was the case, enthusiasts welcomed every additional one, often steadfastly fought for by local groups, with enormous satisfaction. Here, after all, were harbingers of the future. How best could more be brought to birth and into successful operation?

It was felt that a journal could best reflect the new developments, chart moves towards comprehensive schools and unstreaming at primary level and provide encouragement and scope for discussion. Such a journal was launched in the autumn of 1958 by Robin Pedley and me with Jack Walton, a teacher in a local school, later a professor of education in Australia – finally entitled *Forum for the Discussion of New Trends in Education*. Forty years old now, with three issues a year, Forum has recently entered a new phase. Happily a younger editor now has the job which ate largely into my time for over three decades. Without making undue claims, I would say that this journal, by teachers for teachers, was particularly influential during the 1960s and early 1970s when meshed closely with the grain of the times.

While the initial number (September 1958) carried an authoritative article on the progress of the London School Plan, by Raymond King, head of a pioneering London comprehensive, two other heads could report on new trends in Leicestershire. This was the first year of the Leicestershire 'Experiment' in comprehensive education, a two-tier system which attracted much attention. There was also a symposium on science teaching by two comprehensive departmental heads, and a discussion of advanced courses in some secondary modern schools. There was a review by Shena Simon, another by Edward Blishen, founder member of the Forum editorial board and author of the recently published *Roaring Boys*. Besides notices in the educational press, the *Manchester Guardian* accorded the new journal a full leader.

During the 1950s I had steadily acquired experience preparing students to teach, which contributed directly to other work during the decade. By its close it might be said the battle for comprehensive education had to all intents and purposes been won, at the ideological level at least. It remained to get on with the job on the ground.

NOTES

1. L.S. Hearnshaw, *Cyril Burt Psychologist*, London 1979, p241.

5

THE SWINGING SIXTIES, 1960-65

The 1960s were heralded by a Tory victory at the polls in 1959. An overall majority of exactly 100 ensured a full five-year term, though the authority of the Macmillan government waned towards its close. October 1964 saw the re-election of the Labour Party after an interval of thirteen years, with a majority of only 4, increased to 96 after the spring election of 1966. In the summer of 1970 Harold Wilson went again to the country and, unexpectedly, lost, to end the short spell of Labour rule.

In this decade, with a positive move ahead in the matter of the common secondary school, the problems of primary schools came to the fore in a new way. The system by which such schools, where large enough, adopted rigid forms of streaming had spread with extraordinary rapidity, even including young children aged seven or less. This now began to be resisted. The situation was carefully studied by George Freeland – the junior school head who contributed to *New Trends* and joined the Forum board – in his two-stream inner city, effectively slum school. Poring over the marks of his ten-year olds in the 11 plus tests in English and Arithmetic we found this distribution: the A stream children took the first 29 places, the bottom 23 went to the B stream, while of the intervening children four were in the B and five in the A stream.

Such results usually convinced headteachers of the accuracy of their original stream placement. But we asked whether these results might reflect differences in teaching, or, more likely, in the social origin of the children, class background, their age, or, indeed differences in ambience of the two classes, among other extraneous factors . Results might not so much warrant conclusions about innate abilities, runs my contemporary note, 'as simply reflect the inevitable results of streaming' – an early diagnosis of the practice as a self-fulfilling prophecy deriving from analysis of the nature of intelligence testing.

The previous head of this school, recognising the close relationship between educational and social problems, had decided on 'a fundamental educational reorganisation', and unstreamed the third year classes. His successor, Freeland, who had taught in streamed junior schools for over twenty years, but also had become increasingly aware of the deleterious effect, followed this lead. The process of unstreaming completed over the next two years, at Taylor School in Leicester, convinced him of the educational advantages; there were 'no doubts' in his mind 'as to the desirability of non-streaming' he wrote in *New Trends*. As two other Leicester heads soon took this road, the city provided something of a test-bed for a reformed junior school – somewhat to the embarrassment of a Chief Education Officer, Elfed Thomas, who upheld the selective system.

The Forum board had no difficulty in agreeing that modification of present practice should be one of the chief aims of the journal. After all the British Psychological Society, in its 1957 report had come out quite strongly against streaming; pointing especially to its exacerbation of initial differences. The experts had condemned streaming of young children in school as self-validating, a point research was to confirm.

I spent a good deal of time at Taylor School observing teachers dealing with the non-streamed situation, sometimes taking classes myself or assisting with the pupil groups formed. So our recorded experience accumulated. At first George Freeland was the only primary teacher on the Forum board, but he was soon joined by the head of a junior school in Otley, Yorkshire – one who had unstreamed a 320 pupil institution. Other educators, with similar experience, for instance Kenneth Coram and Eric Linfield from junior schools at Stevenage and Fareham in Hampshire, were later to join.

So in the early 1960s this practice, so long taken for granted, had become controversial; though customs die hard and this was no exception. The alert ear of Edward Boyle, Minister of Education from July 1962 to April 1964, caught the sense of controversy. Unusually enough, for a Conservative, he invited the National Foundation for Educational Research to undertake a thorough investigation of the issue in 1963 and, in that same year, appointed the Plowden Committee with a broad brief. This opened up the future of primary education, bringing its whole organisation and character under investigation.

Already a year earlier, in November 1962, Forum had organised its first all-day conference on 'Non-Streaming in the Junior School'. Attended by over 200 teachers it was reported by Edward Blishen (Vol. 5, No. 2). The main speaker was Dr J.C. Daniels (a psychometrist who had helped with my initial critique of intelligence testing), who cited all current research, his own included, of the last three years. The three primary school heads connected with Forum then spoke of their experiences in abolishing streaming. This theme was expanded on at a similar conference in April 1964 where secondary school unstreaming was discussed. This meeting also attracted a large number of participants from all over the country.

Now the pace began to hot up. Forum's editorial board drew up a submission to the Plowden Committee, lengthy but tightly argued. This summarised findings of the most recent researches and advanced proposals for the future.

However, only a tiny minority of junior schools of a size to adopt streaming had eliminated the practice. When the NFER research team started work in 1963/4, there was extreme difficulty in locating fifty unstreamed schools – the minimum required to constitute matched pairs. The Forum board argued for a change which was right against the accepted ethos, and structure, of the vast majority of existing schools.

Clearly the Plowden Committee had to consider this issue. Shortly after submitting our Plowden 'Evidence', an invitation came to present orally these views and submit to further questioning. The editor and two experienced junior school heads

(Freeland and Linfield) took up the opportunity. After a convivial lunch in a restaurant opposite the ministry's Curzon Street headquarters, we made our way to the large, bare room allocated to the committee. We were a little concerned as to the nature of the NFER 'Evidence' – had they rubbished non-streaming we would have been in trouble. Perhaps sensing our concern, Maurice Kogan, the young civil servant acting as secretary to the committee, informed us that the NFER report was ambiguous; it did not come down on either side in the debate. It was to be another six years before the NFER team presented final findings.

Duly fortified we joined the committee to present Forum's evidence. My task was to speak to our main brief, mainly on theoretical issues underlying the controversy, while the heads in turn spoke of experiences on the ground; how they had reorganised their schools and what went on in a new non-streamed situation. The atmosphere was friendly and encouraging – besides committee members others present, presumably as 'assessors', appeared sympathetic; one was John Blackie, a senior schools' inspector. The Chair was Mollie Brearley, principal of the Froebel Institute; Lady Plowden, although present, was taking a day off. All went well until a sharp interrogation was suddenly launched by Professor A.J. Ayer, the well known Oxford philosopher and Wykeham Professor of Logic at the university.

Ayer's questions were penetrating but predictable, no doubt those most in people's minds – would not the bright children suffer, how could the teacher cope with the more backward children and so on. The exchange was good-humoured but extended. I had a sense that almost everyone in the room was hoping that Ayer could be won over. Brearley though apparently thought the exchange had been intense enough for she interrupted to convey that it should end.

This incensed the questioner. Cutting short the interrogation, Ayer rotated deliberately and slowly in his seat, until directly confronting the Chair. 'Do I not have the right', he said very deliberately in a tone of suppressed rage, 'to conduct a full examination on this important issue as I think best?' 'Of course, Professor Ayer', was the reply, it could hardly have been other, 'please carry on'. 'Thank you', said Ayer, and, turning back to me, resumed the examination. Unfortunately memory fails to supply the detail, but the report back to the Forum board suggests he was finally satisfied.

The Plowden Committee, as is well known, did, in fact come out in favour of unstreaming when the report was published three years later, in 1967. Nor did any member voice a reservation on this issue, though there were some on other points. Maybe our *démarche* played its part. As I record this over thirty years on, it occurs that this was the only occasion in my life that I was involved, even if obliquely, in an official policy-making process – leaving aside early participation in the Labour party's Education Advisory Committee. But, as policies have to be made in terms of practicalities – 'the art of the possible' was the phrase Rab Butler liked to use – perhaps an impact at the grass-roots counts, if effective. In any case, where streaming was concerned, it was action in the schools themselves that counted.

The written evidence to Plowden was published in the next issue of Forum, together with a report of our recent conference; this quickly sold out and had to be reprinted. So in October 1964 a small paperback with a similar content, *Non-Streaming in the Junior School*, was advertised in the journal. We were astonished by the response. The first print of 2000 sold out before publication, a second impression issued in November went within a month or two, so a third was required. Within at most six months, at least 10,000 copies of our 'Evidence' to Plowden had been ordered by schools. There could hardly have been a clearer pointer to a sea-change in attitudes, beliefs and aspirations.

At another level, October 1964 was the month the Labour party registered victory in a general election, if only by a whisker, to end thirteen consecutive years of Tory rule. New hopes for the future were abroad, perhaps a new era was in the making. It was a proper moment for a new start in the schools.

Among other work afoot was a study by Brian Jackson of the

Institute of Community Studies. In 1961 he had published research into teachers' attitudes, and his well-designed examination of the whole issue, with which we had been concerned, also appeared in 1964. *Streaming: an educational system in miniature*, grounded on data from a sample of schools of all sizes and types, extremely well written and presented, finally set the seal on streaming. Only a few years ago Brian Jackson died, tragically young, taking part in a run to raise money for a cherished cause. I treasure my copy of his book, which has the inscription: 'Brian Simon: a contribution to a common cause, Brian'. This is also the place to recall the earlier book he and Dennis Marsden published in 1962, *Education and the Working Class*, which contributed largely to the contemporary critique of the grammar school – and so of the selective system generally.

In his 'streaming' book, Jackson records that as late as 1962, one head of a large junior school had maintained that 'not to stream would be the height of professional irresponsibility'. If this accurately reflected the bulk of teacher opinion at the time, by the early 1970s it was hard to find a streamed junior school in the country. (By the time the NFER's research appeared in 1970, three years *after* the Plowden Report, the matter under investigation had become academic.)

To supersede this practice did not, of course, solve all the problems of primary education. What it did was create a new situation, in which the genuine educational problems of young children could at least begin to be tackled and not swept under the carpet through a simplistic categorisation of children on questionable criteria. The new task was to direct research towards the psychology of learning, especially the role of language in mental development, and to facilitate learning in mathematics and science. Research was also needed, we had suggested to Plowden, 'into the whole question of class organisation and teaching method', not least 'the comparative effectiveness of class, group and individual learning situations'. Research should be such as 'to provide a scientific basis for classroom practice'. In sum, to 'move away from rule of thumb teaching' towards 'systematisation of the educational process as a whole' was 'an absolute necessity' to make the most of children's potentialities and so 'equip them to lead satisfying lives'. There is a pointer here to my own research studies of the 1970s, but that is matter for a later chapter.

To return now to the secondary level is to recall that there was not a complete ban on the comprehensive school. In sparsely populated areas, new towns or new suburbs, comprehensive proposals were occasionally accepted. As a handful of towns besides London and Coventry were allowed to go ahead with plans, some new comprehensives surfaced. In due course some concerted moves by local authorities led to the submission of specific plans to the Ministry of Education. The majority were rejected, but this did not quell interest, rather it was a temporary setback.

Forum monitored and reported all this through 1959 and 1960. A series of surveys analysing developments in various parts of the country were begun in South Wales where important innovations were in train. Robin Pedley contributed 'Report from Yorkshire', his home county. Also covered were the West Midlands, Bristol and the West of England, Northumberland and Durham – where affairs sometimes seemed out of sight of Whitehall. In every area there were advances to record, both in terms of new schools established and plans for the future. The first number of Forum's fifth volume in 1962, reserved to the comprehensive school, carried three surveys covering England, Wales and Scotland (showing both the latter to be ahead of England). Raymond King, head of a pioneering London comprehensive, Wandsworth, explained progress in the capital, describing 'a pattern of achievement'. Once more we were inundated with orders and put an immediate reprint in hand.

Another stage can be charted two or three years on in following up the plans of leading local authorities now determined on change. All this preceded the issue of the famous Circular 10/65 by the new Labour government in June 1965. By then Forum had reported a swing to comprehensive education in Bradford and Sheffield, and in Spring 1965 mounting pressure for change in Manchester, Liverpool and Preston, then further large urban authorities and the Lancashire County Council. On the eve of the issue of Circular 10/65 a summary of reorganisation plans by local authorities showed the great bulk were now committed to comprehensive schooling; indeed, were only waiting for the go-ahead. (Forum, Spring 1965)

Finally, in the summer, the Ministry Circular on the reorganisation of secondary education was issued. It *requested* local authorities to submit plans for secondary education – they were not *required* to do so – this would have necessitated legislation. But it was enough to open the floodgates and only a year later comprehensive reorganisation, of a systematic kind, was under way throughout England and Wales, Scotland following a Circular of its own.

Another step towards promoting discussion of the content and conduct of teaching in the early 1960s was to follow up the symposium on Soviet psychology and Luria's little book on speech and mental development in the child. In September 1961 I spent a full month in the Soviet Union assembling, with the help of the Institute of Psychology, papers on educational psychology for another authoritative volume. On this occasion the time was entirely devoted to the work of research institutes in the field of psychology, and I visited those in Moscow, Leningrad, Kiev, Kharkov and Tbilisi. As the first English educationist to visit Georgia, so I was told, I experienced their renowned hospitality, including the ritual of the 'Tabaka'.

Once again there was ready assistance of all kinds, not least from my beloved 'Moscow secretary', Kadriya (Olga) Salimova, helpful at every turn – still a valued friend who visits Leicester. At Luria's suggestion the assembled collection opened with Vygotski's striking paper, 'Learning and Mental Development at School Age', the translation of which he supervised; several versions have since appeared. In this Vygotski clarified his differences with the Swiss philosopher-psychologist Piaget. Other influential papers were by Luria and A.N. Leontiev, while D.B. Elkonin dealt with reading, V.A. Krutetski with mathematics and E.A. Fleshner with physics. The book outlined contemporary evidence underlying an optimistic approach to human potentiality for development, not least in young children usually categorised as 'backward'.

Educational Psychology in the USSR appeared in 1963 (edited jointly with Joan who also translated), and was noticed by the educational and psychological press on both sides of the Atlantic. Meanwhile I recorded my discussions with Soviet psychologists in preparation for a lecture to be delivered to the British Psychological Society at their annual conference at Bristol in 1962. My topic was 'Soviet Psychology and the Learner'. There had been a sudden increase of interest in specialist circles, owing to the publication in the United States of an English version of Vygotski's *Thought and Language*, albeit abridged. Here the initiative had been taken by Jerome Bruner, the well known Harvard psychologist, who became a close friend of Luria and admirer of the work of Vygotski. Bruner's approach signalled a move away from the more determinist standpoint of Piaget and also inspired interest in England. Something of a seismic change was taking place; the new estimation of the potentialities of education constituted a movement of international significance during the 1960s.

The more interesting things become in the present – in university teaching, psychology, renewing school organisation – the more likely it is that thoughts turn to history. Paradoxical though this may seem, historical enquiry may prove a signal means of clarification of current perplexities. I had in hand, after completing a study of English developments to 1870, materials relating to the turn of the twentieth century and beyond. Directly related to current concerns about the promotion of secondary schooling was the Education Act which had launched a new system in 1902. Studying this in its own setting, I had become convinced that this Act, and the administrative measures that went with it, represented a disastrous 'wrong turning' for the English educational system, imposed by a Conservative government with a large majority. The solution imposed was anathema to the numerous nonconformists and to a now increasingly effective Labour movement. I was averse to the unanimous textbook view that the 1902 Act represented a great advance. That hardly accorded with the situation in the 1960s. Another volume began to take shape, bringing to notice for the first time the involvement in educational affairs of the Trade Union Congress, individual unions like the Gasworkers', the nascent Labour and Socialist political organisations, the Independent Labour Party, the Social Democratic Federation and the Socialist League. I also hoped to bring to light the Independent Working Class Education Movement, a rival to the officially respectable Workers' Educational Association. Somehow or other this book was written – it related, of course, to my history lectures to students – to appear as *Education and the Labour Movement*, 1870-1914 (1965).

While the early 1960s tended to be tumultuous at large, there were also problems in the Leicester education department. In 1962 it was fused with the neighbouring Institute of Education. Both institutions being directed by the head of the department, Professor Tibble, no serious difficulties emerged. There was a simple amalgamation of both as the Leicester University School of Education. By this time Leicester had one of the largest post-graduate courses in the country with about two hundred students, attracted partly by the nature of the course and its reputation, but partly by the reflected glory of the Leicestershire authority's two-tier comprehensive plan which appealed to students as innovative. Applications mounted and we could probably have doubled in size had it not been for the barrier of the official quota system. The expansion permitted called for the recruitment of more staff which strengthened the new School of Education in various ways. However, the important transformation, which gave us a lead in the country as a whole and underlined a growing potential, was the unification in this single School of Education, of the original Department and the Institute.

This course was strongly recommended by the 1963 report of the Robbins Committee on Higher Education. Tibble's evidence to the committee, based on experience of the change at Leicester, proved conclusive insofar as universities with institutes were recommended to follow suit. The fusion allowed for a leap forward as a result of amalgamating two differing staffs. The university department had been mostly staffed by 'method' tutors like Bantock, Pedley and myself ; by 1962 the Institute had four or five staff lacking any such responsibility, who lectured to teachers on 'in-service' courses and undertook the research function written into the Institute's constitution. So there was new teaching power for the PGCE course, with the access of such ex-institute staff as Frank Musgrove (sociologist, later Professor of Education at the University of Manchester) and John Eggleston (also a sociologist, later Professor of Education at Keele and Warwick). As a result through the 1960s, the school, with a total full time staff of about thirty-five, could claim expertise in almost every aspect of education, both practical and theoretical.

Internal restructuring followed in the mid-1960s bringing a threefold division of responsibilities, which were getting too complex for a head, the single professor, to control. Since acquiring its Charter in 1956 the University of Leicester taught for, and offered, higher degrees – MAs and Ph.Ds. This function now fell to the School of Education as a new responsibility, very willingly taken on, and the numbers studying for the qualifications rose considerably. While the demand came largely from practising teachers who studied part-time, some full-time MA courses got underway. Geoffrey Bantock, now Reader in Education and shortly to be promoted to a Chair, was asked to take over responsibility in this field. Jack Kerr, science educator and Senior Lecturer, took over responsibility for in-service work with local teachers (which had also expanded considerably), and for relations with local training colleges now strengthened by implementation of the Robbins Committee's proposals relating to a new degree, the B.Ed. While these dispositions were being made, Tibble asked if I would be willing to take over responsibility for the PGCE course, a major undertaking. I had become a 'Reader' in 1964 – a position normally implying a focus on research – but Tibble's proposition meant full involvement in ongoing educational activities among both staff and students. I had learned to combine research with teaching and administration and thought I could continue to do so, so accepted the assignment, in which I had a profound interest, and, by now, some fifteen years experience.

The increased number of students on our PGCE course put local schools under pressure to provide sufficient practice places for them in the Easter term. As a result of this we had split the course some years earlier into two sections, operating independently and sending students into the schools at different times. This kind of 'Box and Cox' system allowed for the more efficient use of resources (at university and schools) and prevented the course becoming a mass affair with large lecture audiences and classes. The Leicester principle of small group work, which Tibble greatly favoured, continued to predominate despite increased numbers. For several years in the late 1950s and early 1960s I looked after one of these sections (A) and Robin Pedley the other (B); that is up to 1963, when he left to take up the directorship of the Exeter Institute of Education. Others, of course, took over Pedley's responsibilities at Leicester.

I found responsibility for the whole PGCE course rewarding. In addition to the two sections A and B there was also a small, experimental section (C), though this tended to generate difficult problems. But it was necessary to pass on my direct responsibility for section A to focus on teacher training activities as a whole, involving nearly two hundred students in three sections – almost an institution in itself. This whole reorganisation was an adjustment at university level to encompass the upward thrust of schools – and especially the new demands deriving from the swing to comprehensive education, by now well under way in Leicestershire – the main area where our students undertook their school practice.

By this time Leicester was developing an innovatory system whereby experienced teachers acted as 'teacher-tutors' (or today, 'mentors') to students when on teaching practice, so sharing the task with the university's 'Method tutors'. This approach proved of great value during the transition to comprehensive education since new issues relating to teaching and learning were arising in the schools themselves, and it was the experienced teachers in the schools who were in the best position to induct trainee teachers into the new situation. The new comprehensive schools now coming into being generously offered to take several students for practice, also permitting several of their senior staff to act as teacher-tutors (for which they received an honorarium). This turn towards school-focussed training, though retaining a close link with the university, proved productive, while the linkage of a large number of teacher-tutors with the university's own tutors further bonded the university with the leading primary and secondary schools in the area. So we benefited in several ways from these new developments. Overseeing this relationship, promoting what appeared positive, was, now, part of my job. The future, in the mid-1960s, looked bright.

6

THE SWINGING SIXTIES, 1966-1970

There were 262 comprehensive secondary schools in England and Wales in 1965, educating 8.5 per cent of pupils in the maintained school sector. The following year the Labour government went to the polls with a programme guaranteeing support for the single secondary school, and increased a tenuous majority of four into one exceeding ninety. The pledge was redeemed with the issue of Circular 10/66, and rapid expansion in comprehensive education ensued. Leicestershire became the first English county to abolish 11 plus selection in 1969, and other counties soon followed. In 1970 there were 1250 comprehensive schools educating 32 per cent of all children of secondary age in maintained schools. An accompaniment to the rise of the new schools was an enlargement of educational work at the university level, including publications and research concerned with educational reform.

Part of the credit for the realisation of the single secondary school belongs to the Comprehensive Schools Committee (CSC) – an effective pressure group in the classic sense. Established in the autumn of 1965 its chief object was to assist local authorities first to make plans (as requested in Circular 10/65) then to implement them. Sponsors included Peter Townsend, Angus Wilson, Lionel Elvin, Brian Jackson, Michael Young (later Lord Young of Dartington), Robin Pedley and myself. But the dynamic energy was generated by Caroline Benn who, under the modest title 'Information Officer', turned her home into a powerhouse of intelligence on local authority policy all over the country.

The need for a critical body of the kind was soon apparent. Local authority plans had now to be submitted to the Department of Education and Science (DES) for approval. Some of the early decisions provoked hostility: schemes which could be categorised as 'fully comprehensive', such as that at Liverpool, were rejected, while less thorough plans found acceptance. A key issue was the acceptance by the DES of the Doncaster Plan, which embodied a system of 'guided parental choice' and placement of children at the age of thirteen in different but 'parallel' types of school – not a genuinely comprehensive system. The matter was raised in the first number of the bulletin issued by the Comprehensive Schools Committee; the attention this received in the press was a sign of lively public interest. Forum, which continued to produce reports on developments in education, carried an analysis – 'Social Selection and the Doncaster Plan' (Vol. 8, 1966). It assessed the role of the DES and called on the Secretary of State, Anthony Crosland, to rethink his decision to support a 'less-than-comprehensive' system in the Doncaster Plan.

The Comprehensive Schools Committee continued to monitor the transition to a comprehensive system, linking up local authorities, answering queries and maintaining the pressure for ordered change. A regular feature was its annual survey covering every local authority's plans. Forum meanwhile turned especially to the internal organisation of developing schools, particularly the issue of streaming at the secondary stage. Three joint conferences organised jointly with CSC – in 1966, 1967 and 1970 – dealt with this key question of streaming, sixth forms, and 'Teachers for Comprehensive Schools' respectively. But the DES recognition of partially reorganised schools as 'comprehensive' remained a problem – as successive issues of Forum underline – with articles now often contributed by experienced comprehensive heads, not least in London and Coventry.

London led the way towards a rational form of school organisation but at the same time had major problems with which to contend. Figures from the summer of 1969 show that very few Inner London Education Authority's (ILEA) schools could be called genuinely comprehensive and that 19 per cent of eleven-year-olds still sat an 11+ examination for entry into grammar schools. The problem was the continued existence of a large number of voluntary-aided grammar schools, for the most part under the control of religious bodies, which refused to participate in the general movement. By contrast a school head from Coventry wrote that there were still 'no genuinely comprehensive schools' in the area, which was attributed to the continued existence of two large direct-grant grammar schools. Legislation was required to alter this situation.

It could reasonably be argued that, with the decision at national level to supercede a harmful form of selection and progress locally towards this end, it was past time for decisions directed to realising policy. One contribution was a short bill, drawn up by Caroline Benn, facing up to the legal difficulties perceived as potential obstacles to fully comprehensive schooling. Eventually in 1969 the Government's bill was published, but it came to nothing as the election of 1970 supervened. There remained the achievement on the ground floor: the comprehensive movement had developed an impetus of its own.

The next step was to provide a reference library, and books were planned to appeal to and inform a wider audience of developments under way, and under threat. Enrolment at colleges of education had increased three-fold in accordance with recommendations of the Robbins Report – they were now attended by over 100,000 students. Students in the 1960s showed a lively interest in new developments, and *The Evolution of the Comprehensive School, 1926-1969*, written with David Rubinstein, an experienced comprehensive teacher in London, was published as part of the Students Library of Education series. Revised in 1973, with a total print-run of some 15,000 copies, this book aroused the interest of a new generation.

A great deal more onerous was a request from publisher, McGraw Hill for an authoritative review of the transition to comprehensive education up until 1967. I was ready to entertain the idea on one condition – that it would be jointly authored with Caroline Benn. It would have been an impossible task single-handed, and Caroline Benn knew a great deal more about local authority plans and functioning comprehensive schools than anyone else, the Department of Education and Science included. Committed to the movement, she was also ready to take on the heavy load involved. The outcome was *Half-way There. Report on the British Comprehensive School Reform* (1970).

During the year following the publication of Circular 10/65 the Public School Commission, chaired by Professor David Donnison (a strong proponent of comprehensive reorganisation), considered a proposal to integrate the semi-independent direct-grant schools into local comprehensive systems. The immediate situation called for a bold initiative. If the new schools were prepared to seize their opportunities, learn from the changes in primary education and adopt more flexible structures, much might be achieved. On the other hand, if the new schools were to be rigidly streamed, and the children divided into a set of hierarchical teaching groups, the whole purpose of making the change to comprehensive education might be subverted. At this point, four hundred teachers packed into the main hall of the London Institute of Education for a Forum/CSC conference on non-streaming. Chaired by the venerable London head, Raymond King, three experienced heads of well-known comprehensives described, analysed and commended procedures in restructuring on the foundation of more flexible grouping of younger children. An intense interest was also apparent during the ensuing discussion, but it was the afternoon session that produced an unforgettable impression. This time long-service class teachers and departmental heads led the way. The star was Derek Roberts, Head of Geography at the David Lister Comprehensive in Hull, whose talk was not only deeply humanist but well illustrated and very practical. The conference warmed to him in a way seldom seen; the highly professional approach was particularly appreciated. Other heads of department and class teachers were also adept in sharing experiences. Summing up this conference, as editor of Forum, I could pass on a promise to forward this cause, from a meeting which placed the feasibility of mixed ability teaching at the early secondary stage on the map.

In October 1966 the Gloucestershire local authority organised a similar conference chaired by the Chief Education Officer (Milroy) at which Jack Walton, now Head of Beaminster School, Dorset, was the main speaker. In November the Nottingham Institute of Education had an extraordinary response to a teach-in, attracting over three hundred teachers, administrators and councillors. This was chaired by Harry Davies, once a grammar school head and now a professor of education, assisted by John Daniels, with Derek Roberts and several others contributing teaching experience. At Exeter University there was a three day residential course, addressed by Robin Pedley, Jack Walton and Derek Roberts, this time on the crucial issue of the pedagogy of teaching unstreamed groups; another large conference was held at Redland College of Education, Bristol, and another at York University, organised by my old friend Harry Rée, Professor of Education there and another former grammar school head. Elsewhere working parties were set up by teachers to move the whole discussion on.

It was at this point that the Conservative party became increasingly concerned about these activities, and their longer term implications. In *The Making of Tory Education Policy in Post-War Britain, 1950-1986*, Christopher Knight writes of 'preservationists' in the Party (basically traditionalists) being increasingly angered by the 'Heath-Boyle' line – seen as soft on new developments. They were also 'disturbed by "intelligence" collected by the Conservative Research Department (CRD)' concerning the activities of 'Marxist educationists' whose aim was defined as 'the destruction of the tripartite system of secondary schooling – particularly the elimination of streaming'. Characteristically no news had reached the CRD of the rising interest among students, teachers and local authorities in moves to extricate the national system of schooling from a dead end, from a form of organisation which actively prevented the raising of standards required, as Boyle had recognised. Attention concentrated instead on supposed rabble-rousers among whom

Professor Brian Simon was allotted a key role as 'a leading spirit of the educational left' and 'key figure' in the campaign 'to abolish selection in all its forms' – although 'left-wing sympathisers were also said to be at large' in the Institutes of Education.

In reality, the questioning of 11 plus selection and advocacy of non-streaming came from within schools and was most effectively discussed – in both negative and positive terms – by practising teachers. Discussion of this order could not have been engineered from outside, or imposed, least of all could it be ascribed to a single individual. What is really remarkable is the extent to which experienced professionals were prepared to adapt or rethink time-honoured teaching methods and organisational forms to meet the pressures and promises of changing times.

What was encouraging however was the extent to which suggestions and proposals came into Forum from primary schools, to be considered by a Board including several primary heads and teachers. All over the country primary schools were rejecting streaming and moving in unison to non-streamed structures. Early in 1966 I was deputed to conduct a mini-observational study of non-streamed teaching; this was reported in 'Anatomy of the Non-Streamed Classroom: teaching non-streamed classes in the Junior School' (Forum, Vol. 8, No. 3, 1966).

Five classes were observed in two non-streamed junior schools in or close to Leicester – two of these were whole class teaching lessons, the others based on group or individual work. I observed that no specific difficulties seemed to arise, either in the whole class teaching situation or in that utilising group and individual work. Also significant was the importance of recognising the *variety* of responses to the non-streamed situation: some teachers stressed individualisation as the main principle of organisation, but this varied between tightly controlled and systematised individual work to a more permissive, unstructured situation. Again those focusing on group work also operated in diverse ways, groups being either fixed for all activities or highly mutable, changing their composition for different activities. It was all too clear that a thorough investigation was required, as Forum had informed the Plowden Committee. Teachers of non-streamed classes had shown great ingenuity and professional skill in solving problems arising from the change; their pioneering work needed underpinning and the support of relevant scientific investigation.

There was also a reorientation of approach to educational studies at this time, originating at a conference in 1963 at which the lead was taken by Richard Peters, Professor of the Philosophy of Education at the London Institute. He was the chief proponent of a rigorous treatment of education for teachers as an alternative to what he labelled the 'undifferentiated mush' characterising colleges and university departments of education. One outcome of the Robbins Report of 1963 was the introduction of a four-year Bachelor of Education degree for selected college students. At issue, therefore, was the content of the higher grade course to be introduced. The proposal was that education, not itself a 'subject' in the normal academic sense, could only be rigorously treated if approached along specific academic lines; that is by way of studying its contributing disciplines: psychology, sociology, history of education, and above all philosophy. A means of realising this objective was the formation of the Students Library of Education, handled by Routledge and Kegan Paul and, specifically, Brian Southam. This was duly classified in four sections, though an 'education' section also attained a small entry. In all around eighty short studies resulted, in both hardback and paperback.

There was an editorial board chaired by J.W. Tibble, Professor of Education and Head of the School of Education at Leicester University, an active proponent of the plan, though himself an educationist before anything else. Then, originally, a representative of each of the four main disciplines seen as intrinsic to serious educational studies. These were Richard Peters (philosophy), William Taylor (sociology, he then held a Chair at Bristol), and Ben Morris (psychology, also a Bristol professor). In the absence of an interest in education in university history departments, I was invited to speak for the history of education, and although no academic historian, and doubting aspects of the 'four discipline' approach (where was pedagogy, for instance, the 'science of teaching'?), an opportunity was offered to press the claims of an historical approach to understanding educational theory and practice not to be missed.

The board meetings, later joined by another philosopher, Paul Hirst, were lively and stimulating and I undoubtedly gained from the discussions. The first major production was *The Study of Education* (1966), a volume in which all set out their wares, it might be said, but which also articulated the rationale of the initiative. Over the next decade or so this book sold a total of some 20,000 copies, mainly in universities and colleges, and put education more securely on the map. Otherwise it was my job to seek out authors and handle manuscripts as they came in.

The historical section of the library got off to a good start with some twenty books in a decade. The Professor of Education at Sheffield, W.H.G. Armytage, ever energetic and with a wide-ranging knowledge, contributed four studies of American, French, German and Russian influence on English education which united the historical and comparative approach. Malcolm Seaborne and Gerald Bernbaum (both from Leicester) also contributed on local and contemporary studies respectively, but I was especially glad to gain as authors Eric Eaglesham, John Lawson, R.J.W. Selleck, Harold Silver and James Murphy, all noted for earlier work in the education field. A co-editor of Forum, Nanette Whitbread, contributed a best-seller with her *Evolution of the Nursery-Infant School* (1972).

The Students Library marked a specific phase in the study of education, one laid low by the cold winds of the 1980s. The failure to find a place for 'methods of teaching', and the elimination of pedagogy from the outset, was an inherent weakness in the initial conception; nor could this be overcome by introducing, under Hirst, some books on method. By the early 1980s the stress was on the preparation of teachers as skilled practitioners. In short, a failure to relate effectively theory and practice proved the Achilles' heel of an over-specialist, essentially divided approach, which into the bargain failed to satisfy educationists such as Tibble himself. With his death a few years later his place was taken by my old Cambridge tutor, Lionel Elvin, recently retired as Director of the London Institute. But the times were no longer propitious and the fortunes of the Students Library waned. Does anyone read these books today?

In *The Study of Education* I argued straightforwardly for the overriding importance of the historical approach. The sense that things can change, have done so in the past and will in the future, can liberate the teacher from determination by current conditions. In becoming a professional teacher the student enters, as a small cog, a vast and highly organised machine. This may induce both a sense of helplessness and of fatalism. With a background of historical study there can be, even for the beginner, a detached or critical awareness of the place of existing procedures in teaching and administrative structures. Although there is limited scope within a one year (PGCE) course, there is clearly room for discussion to awaken curiosity and extend understanding by historical study. Later more opportunity is offered by in-service courses or private reading to profit from an induction.

For various reasons there was a sudden upsurge of interest in the history of education in the late 1960s. Its scope widened from the often arid narratives of the past which had tended to focus on 'acts and facts'. A new link was cultivated with the burgeoning field of social history and sociology which meant that even more relevant work resulted. With the rapid expansion of teacher education at universities and colleges, more and more people were now professionally involved, and those taking higher degrees increased to enrich the field. In 1968 philosophers of education formed their own association, and historians determined to do likewise. Owing to the energetic efforts of David Bradshaw, principal of a further education college – inspired by work for a doctorate under Harry Armytage – a founding conference was called at Liverpool in 1969. Attracting nearly two hundred, this conference decided to launch the History of Education Society. David Bradshaw acted as first president, a job to which I succeeded in 1972 for three very happy years. Nearly thirty years on the society still flourishes, holding bi-annual conferences and publishing both a journal and a bulletin. In particular it has formed valuable links abroad after conferences in France, Germany, Spain, Portugal and Poland.

Individual studies of the history of English education have tended to concentrate on the nineteenth century, but some have contributed to an understanding of early modern developments, during the 'renaissance' and the Reformation. Among works written for the education of teachers early in the twentieth century, and still read, are those of W.H. Woodward, whose interest extended to discussion of pedagogical practice in Europe; to the work of Budé and Cordier, Vives and Melanchthon. Latterly contributions from the history of education – Kenneth Charlton, *Education in Renaissance England* (1965) and Joan Simon, *Education and Society in Tudor England* (1966) – have filled a gap in Tudor studies. There have been many additions to knowledge of the nineteenth century, not least two books drawn from doctoral theses which cover the legislation which fostered a 'public schools' system with particular links with Oxford and Cambridge colleges: David Allsobrook, *Schools for the Shires* (1986) and Colin Shrosbree, *The Public Schools and Private Education: the Clarendon Commission 1861-64 and the Public Schools Act* (1988).

The new interest in local studies, a speciality at Leicester, has contributed notably to the cultivation of the history of schools serving local communities. On arrival in Leicestershire in 1950 I was immediately impressed by discovery of seventeenth-century schoolhouses in market towns and villages across the county, and embarked, with Joan Simon, on a county-wide survey, with the notable work of W.G. Hoskins as guide. The outcome was *Education in Leicestershire, 1540-1940* (1968), a collection of studies by several authors which opens with sixteenth and seventeenth century developments.

Most of the market towns of the county, we had discovered, had a grammar school serving the local community. At Market Harborough the seventeenth-century school building (on stilts leaving space for market stalls beneath) still blazons puritan messages, painted under the eaves. Other old schools were also to be found at Market Bosworth, where Samuel Johnson taught, at Ashby-de-la-Zouch, Wymondham and Leicester itself; a history of the latter was written by Claire Cross, a pupil of Wyggeston girls' school, and now a professor of history at York. Then we discovered subscription books, dating from 1620, which every intending teacher had to sign to signal readiness to uphold the doctrine of the established church, or subscribe to the 39 Articles in order to gain a license to teach. In successive books are the signed inscriptions of seventeenth-century Leicestershire schoolmasters – stating name, qualification (whether graduate or not) and the school in which they taught – providing proof of continuity and length of service of schools and masters; and not only in the market towns, but as it turned out, also in larger villages (these usually being non-graduates). Finally, a search through the registers of four Cambridge colleges – which provide information about all entrants, school of origin, master's name and father's occupation – enabled a picture to be drawn of a system in action, serving the county community.

Of particular interest in this connection was the extent to which educational provision was linked with other public services – such as the upkeep of bridges and highways – through embryonic forms of local government, and the extent of local democratic control; developments stemming from Reformation legislation. One locally administered school, Melton Mowbray, was often in trouble with authority for holding school in the church as no building had been provided here; but the practice continued through to the eighteenth century. Local involvement was evident through to the mid-nineteenth century when the master was still elected by a popular gathering of all who chose to attend; a 'tumultary assembly' as a shocked official once described it. Schoolmasters evidently recruited assistants themselves – if one scribbled note discovered among the archives is representative. This particular writer was schoolmaster at Frisby-on-the-Wreake, a populous village in the fertile Wreake valley, his note addressed to an archdeaconry official.

I hold it convenient and requisite to have one or other in Frisby to teach petty boys, and prepare them for me; I think none so fitting as the bearer hereof Edward Bennet so I pri'thee do him and me the favour that he may be licensed and you shall command your truly loving friend and servant, Anthony Rawson, schoolmaster of Frisby.

Here was a graduate master teaching a village school, operating in embryonic form a system of recruitment that still, essentially, obtains.

So little has been generally known about the conduct of local schools on the ground – as against endless recital of acts or regulations to control development – that 'a grammar school in every town' can be presented as a novel idea of the 1990s; and there are those at Westminster who look on local control of schools, even elected local authorities, as a dangerous innovation. But to return from seventeenth-century Leicestershire to the provision of teachers for twentieth-century schools, the development of historical and other research contributed markedly to the life of Leicester School of Education. There was also the asset of the 'Leicestershire plan' with its abolition of 11 plus, which further attracted students so that the school was inundated with applications. According to the Graduate Teacher Training Registry (our clearing house), Leicester and one other modern university department (leave aside the ancient universities), were continually the most sought after. It only needed the addition of special distinction in 'the study of education' (linked to the name of our director Tibble), provided unexpectedly by a Sunday broadsheet which had conducted an enquiry into the speciality of each university.

A new regime was established with Tibble's retirement in 1966, when a revolving directorship of the school was introduced; each of the three heads responsible for specific areas acting as director in turn. There were lengthy discussions in a top university committee before the then revolutionary step was taken, for what was a very new School of Education. This also involved creating two new professors – that is, Jack Kerr and myself – as Geoffrey Bantock already held a chair. In future the directorship passed at two-year intervals between the members of what was sometimes called the Troika. The system worked well enough for us though it was not fully sustained in later years. My first stint was 1968 – 70 during the 'student revolt' and the next lasted three years, 1974-77.

It was not until I took up my directorship that I came to know at first hand how crucial committees running the academic side of the university operated. As is the case with most civic universities, academic affairs are the province of the Senate which meets monthly during term time and consists largely of professors who, up to the mid 1960s, were also normally heads of department. The business, financial and administrative control of such universities is in the hands of the Council, which includes lay members and to which Senate reports – a structure with which I was familiar at second hand given a father who had been successively Treasurer and then Chairman of Council of Manchester University. Senate affairs had gradually become familiar, for three members of a small body of 24 were elected to represent 'non-professorial staff'. After some years I became one of these. We took the responsibility seriously, reporting back to a constituency comprising the bulk of the academic staff and occasionally working out an agreed line on some controversial issue. As professors on Senate probably did not discuss matters among themselves in this way, this procedure, on occasions, gave us something of an advantage.

Promotion to a Chair automatically brings full membership of Senate. But to be director of the school (corresponding to the Deans of other faculties) also brought membership of the 'Establishment Board', a committee of about ten which dealt with every academic matter arising which required decision. This board also made, and controlled, all new appointments, though normally co-opting members of the specific department concerned. Most large universities devolve this latter responsibility to Faculty Board, even departments. At Leicester, in my time at least, all appointments were kept firmly, through the Establishment Board and Senate, in the hands of the university as a whole. The board, of course, reported to Senate where any decision could be challenged, though few were.

There were many appointments during my periods of membership – owing to uninterrupted expansion and the creation of important faculties such as engineering and medicine – so attendance at board meetings became almost a way of life, on top of all other responsibilities that went with the job. Nevertheless discussions were consistently interesting, touching on the problems and character of other departments and giving an all-round view of the university's function. One of the main responsibilities of the Board was to deal with recommendations for promotion – mainly to Senior Lectureships and Readerships, but also to Chairs. These provoked endless discussion, as can be imagined, since so much depended on the outcomes, in terms of career opportunities and the university's reputation. Business which could involve delicate matters was dealt with very fairly; normally a consensus would be arrived at after very lengthy and indeed repeated discussion. This could be seen as a good example of academic self-government, and indeed the university prided itself on keeping administrative costs low – a smaller proportion of its total income went on administration than in most other universities. From my experience of this and other committees, I would say that Leicester was a well organised university, one in which resources were seen to be fairly shared out (another responsibility) and the staff generally found life and work congenial. But I retired, of course, before government policies forced 'economies' and correspondingly new procedures on higher education as a whole.

As the 1960s drew to a close, however, there were some dramatic, even ominous, events. Leicester took the brunt of the early students' revolt, which characterised this period when I was Director of the School of Education. There was cause to sympathise with some students' demands – for instance, for representation on Senate and Faculty Boards, which, after all, the NUS had called for thirty years earlier. Where the staff differed from students was in their analysis of universities as arms of an oppressive state, requiring overthrow, or with some of the tactics pursued, though there was little violence at Leicester. After some changes, including accepting student representation on Senate, Faculty Boards and other committees, matters reverted to normality.

A direct result of the student revolt was the appearance in 1969 of the first of a series of 'Black Papers' on education. These opened with virulent attacks on students but soon transferred fire to developments in primary and comprehensive schools, with the clear objective of rubbishing contemporary developments. At the time supporters of progressive developments perhaps under-estimated the significance of the attack, given faith in the indestructibility of the advances made; only after several years did destructive criticism begin to bite.

There was a third unexpected occurrence. Against all predictions, including national opinion polls, the general election of June 1970 returned an overall Tory majority of about thirty; and, as Ted Heath formed his government, Margaret Thatcher emerged as Education Secretary. As Heath had previously pronounced comprehensive education to be acceptable, it did not seem the transition was at risk, though still at an early stage of development.

1970 was also the year, it may be remembered, that saw publication of *Halfway There. Report on the British Comprehensive School Reform.* This book was more widely reviewed and aroused more interest than any other with which I was involved; not merely in the national and educational press but in the provinces, for many local newspapers picked out information relevant to their areas. In retrospect 1970 marked the peak of the movement launched in the early 1960s. Little could be done by even so determined a politician as Margaret Thatcher to stop, or even slow down, what she herself dubbed a 'roller coaster'. Both conservative and labour local authorities were now realising long gestated plans. The official (DES) count of comprehensive schools in England and Wales for that year stood at 1250, catering for a third, 32 per cent, of all pupils in maintained secondary schooling. After four years of Heath's government comprehensive schools numbered over 3000, taking in just short of 70 per cent. Evidently *Half-Way There* celebrated the point when the swing to comprehensive schooling accelerated.

It is good to remember the three years work with Caroline Benn; cooperation was harmonious and all our targets met. Besides bearing the major brunt of the writing she designed the crucial questionnaire, which allowed for computer analysis and provided the bulk of the data for the book. Analyses were made available primarily by our assistant, Guy Neave, who had access to a computer – much less common in those days. My main task was to review the organisation of the curriculum and the patterns of functioning comprehensive schools. Caroline contributed thirteen chapters covering local authority schemes, various types of emerging comprehensive school, together with administration, relations with the home, issues of 'choice' and the neighbourhood school. Thirty recommendations framed as a future guide provided the conclusion.

Partnership with the wife of a cabinet minister had its lighter moments and there are one or two references to the point in Tony Benn's diary of the day. As it turned out, publication of the book coincided with the election and due to a newspaper strike, the BBC were the only organisation who could be approached for widespread publicity. However, as Tony Benn's diary protested, the BBC 'declined, in reviewing the book, to mention Caroline's name because she is the wife of a minister; it is so offensive'. The lack is then supplied by recognition of the 'enormous effort' jointly put into the book which 'will be studied all over'. It was certainly reviewed in a manner suggesting an impact: 'The most important and detailed book yet published on comprehensive education in Britain', according to *The Times*. It would be succeeded in 1996 by *Thirty Years On*, this time by Caroline in conjunction with Clyde Chitty, editor of Forum; a progress report which, once more, stands in for what governments have failed to do.

One downbeat point must be added before closing with the 1960s: the new thrust given to IQ by Arthur Jensen in 1969. In fact he contributed what became a celebrated article – 'How Much Can We Boost IQ and Scholastic Achievement?' – to a relatively obscure academic journal early in 1969. Here he maintained that both racial and social class differences in intelligence were genetically determined, that at least 80 per cent of the variance in intelligence was due directly to heredity. Public resources devoted to compensatory education – the then Headstart programme in the USA, for instance – were deemed to be a waste of money. Jensen argued that a new approach was required based on psychometric analysis.

This caused a furore in the United States, being hotly contested by social scientists, geneticists and educationists alike. The thesis immediately made front pages in Britain – it was usually presented as controversial rather than an exposition of the latest scientific knowledge. But the two Black Papers of 1969 included articles by H.J. Eysenck, Cyril Burt and Richard Lynn who *all* generally accepted the Jensen thesis, giving it currency in Britain and stressing the implications in terms of the desirability of selection and streaming. Clearly there were new battles over old ground to come.

7

THE 1970S: A TURN TO PEDAGOGY AND RESEARCH

In a sense, efforts to establish a single secondary school rooted in a local community, to make this level of schooling a reality for all children, could seem like a restoration of a traditional pattern. But once that objective moved towards a modern realisation, new matters called for careful attention. Techniques of teaching and forms of inner school organisation both needed transformation to meet new potentials; schools with a comprehensive intake and a new outlook needed autonomous and reflective teachers ready to set the standards in relation to the successful learning experience of pupils. This meant the end of the perception of the teacher as 'instructor'; to get as many as possible through the 11 plus at primary stage and make a good showing in GCE for a proportion of 16 year olds. In this connection the new development of school-based teacher-tutors was encouraging, forging constructive bonds between schools and teacher-training departments. More teacher participation at this point was essential since only teachers firmly based in the new schools understood how best to realise the opportunities opening up.

To encourage this development and clarify the new skills and qualities required by teachers in the new schools, Forum, in co-operation with the Comprehensive School Committee, ran a well-attended conference in the summer of 1970, addressed by experienced heads (Pat Daunt, Roy Waters), and teachers.

Indeed from this point the partnership between schools and training institutions began to develop on a national scale. This was one crucial feature of the new movement; the swing to the single secondary school that now swept the country.

There was another issue which emerged as local authorities finalised plans – precisely what population the new schools should serve. This question has since become highly controversial, but the early schools were designed with the clear objective of serving the local neighbourhood – some as 'community schools'. Traditionally this was always the objective of the movement. The clear advantages of this approach were emphasised in Forum/CSC's 1971 conference at which heads from well-established schools in Sheffield and Bristol stressed the vital importance of building a close and intimate relationship between the school and its immediate neighbourhood – a relationship which could not have been achieved in the divided system.

With quality of learning for all pupils now at the centre of attention, examinations required adjustment. It may be recalled that at this time GCE 'O' level was designed for the top 20 per cent of pupils, CSE (Certificate of Secondary Education) for the next 40 per cent, the remaining pupils being left in an 'exam-free' limbo. This system forced divisions between pupils and so clashed with the ideals of the new schools which aimed to educate all. A Forum/CSC conference in 1973 called for a single examination for all at 16, an objective that was to be realised in course of time, but not for twelve long years ahead, to the detriment of thousands of secondary boys and girls. In the interim new schools on the way to comprehensive reorganisation suffered an overall external constriction which checked successful development not only for pupils but for teachers too.

In 1974 another important development was taken up. The conference that year examined how the main principles of comprehensive education might be extended to cover the entire 16-19 age range – where old divisions were most firmly established. New perspectives had also to be considered with the establishment of successful tertiary colleges (spanning the academic-vocational divide) in various parts of the country. My summing up on this occasion stressed the need for 'variety in a context of wholeness', with the aim of unifying developments to provide common educational experiences for all.

Changes gathered pace in schools of the 1970s and by 1974 new versions of an old set of ideas re-surfaced. The first of these was the theory that schools could do little or nothing to alter differences between children said to arise from their individual social (and class) backgrounds. The idea derives from social scientists in the United States and is grounded in statistical techniques. It was claimed that schools exacerbated initial inequalities. This was a determinist view bringing in question the whole comprehensive reform, preaching that schools 'make no difference'. At the same time there was also a revival of the classic IQ theories of the past – again an American phenomenon.

A special number of Forum (Spring 1974) asserted the opposite – 'Schools CAN make a Difference' – with critical analyses of the ideas and research underlying the assertions of social scientists. These views also led directly to the schools' effectiveness movement, which still flourishes, though not always to good effect. Subsequent research in Britain has shown just how much difference schools can make and research turned to discovering why and how. But in the 1970s the immediate need was to contest the defeatist message coming from the USA. It was the old story again; the theoretical helplessness conveyed by this message could lead to a fatalism which elicits a self-fulfilling prophecy. Teachers, once presented with data purporting to highlight their inability to enhance human development through education, might be more likely to give up. In a striking article, Patrick Meredith, Professor of Psychology at the University of Leeds, strongly rebutted this renewed assault of the intelligence testers (Arthur Jensen and H.J. Eysenck) (Forum, Vol. 16, No.2).

The second threat came from 'the new sociology' popular at the time in Britain. Essentially the proponents of this view, expressed in an Open University Reader, *Knowledge and Control* by Michael F. D. Young, advanced a relativist view of knowledge and pointed to the oppressive character of 'repressive middle class culture'. While Young moved away from this position within a few years, his views remained influential, especially among young radical teachers in the London area. The standpoint of 'new' sociologists was subjected to sharp criticism in Forum by Olive Banks – a respected 'mainstream' sociologist – and by Joan Simon, whose penetrating points drew a telephone call from Basil Bernstein, of the London Institute, to join a discussion of the issues in a seminar. Then *the* leading educational sociologist, Bernstein also distanced himself from Young's relativism. But this remained an important issue in any serious discussion of the content of education, and indeed overall objectives, of comprehensive schooling.

In 1973 Forum took another initiative, with the pamphlet *Indictment of Margaret Thatcher, Secretary of State 1970-73*. Also by Joan Simon, this exposed a series of arbitrary actions by the secretary of state, recalling the contemporary indictment of the President of the United States over Watergate. At the time several local authorities were considering legal action to negate decisions regarded as unjust and probably illegal; throughout the early summer of 1973 Thatcher had set about emasculating comprehensive proposals, evoking a tide of anger up and down the country. The Forum indictment detailed the cases and mode of treatment. There was a response of sorts from the Secretary of State, at a discussion held with young teachers from inner-city secondary schools. One teacher present was a former Leicester PGCE student, Clyde Chitty, who, at a time when such courses were being sharply criticised, observed that he had 'gained greatly from attending seminars on comprehensive schooling organised by Professor Brian Simon'. Was the Secretary of State familiar with his work? 'Oh yes', replied Thatcher (through what seemed gritted teeth). 'We know all about Brian Simon here'.

As a postscript to this reported exchange, there is the comment of Adrian Woodbridge in the mid 1990s, after a five-page summary of my outlook; 'although Simon was on the far left of British politics, he was at the forefront of the sweep in post-war educational thought' and, by the early 1970s, 'much of the educational establishment was to accept his conclusions'. This reference to publications of the 1950s (and later) occurs in *Measuring the Mind, Education and Psychology c1860-1990* (1994, pp 295-300), by an historian with a wholehearted belief that psychometry has made a valuable contribution to education. It would have been of more use to turn attention to all the relevant data and recognise how far new ideas derived from teachers at all levels of the system.

1972 saw the revised edition of *Half-Way There* and a second edition of *The Evolution of the Comprehensive School*; but also realisation of a long-cherished project which contributed an historical background to current moves for educational reform. The book in question was *The Radical Tradition in Education in England*, a set of readings to complement my first historical volume covering the period 1780-1870. This presented writings on education by radical democrats from the early nineteenth century, up to William Morris – names which should be familiar to all educationists are those of William Godwin, Thomas Paine, Robert Owen, Richard Carlile, Robert Dale Owen, William Thompson and William Lovett. But many of their writings have been long out of print and hard to find, though they remain astonishingly relevant to modern concerns.

Another move to historical investigation was related directly to current interest in the structure of schooling and pedagogy. My paper 'Classification and Streaming: a study of grouping in English Schools, 1860-1960', from *History and Education*, (Paul Nash ed., Random House, 1970), covered the pre-history of streaming up to World War One, through the inter-war period when its ideological (or theoretical) justification began to be established, to the dominance of mental testing in the 1950s. As discussion extended to the decline of the practice and the theoretical dominance of testing, this paper turned out to be a case study of the emergence and decline of a particular pedagogic practice.

It also proved useful when I turned back to my historical series, to a projected third and final volume covering 1920 to 1970. However, once again, matters did not work out as originally planned. In 1968 the fifty-year-rule – the embargo on all public records for half a century – was suddenly reduced to a mere thirty years. At a stroke all public records, covering the entire inter-war period, became available. So rich was the material I quarried at the Kew Public Record Office – an ideal spot for research – that in the outcome I decided, whether rightly or not, to focus specifically on a study of that precise period. The outcome was a kind of case study in educational stagnation, but none-the-less interesting as such. The period was fraught with political conflict so that the eventual title was *The Politics of Educational Reform, 1920-1940*. A particular source adding interest to the analysis was the discovery of a full list of R.H. Tawney's *Manchester Guardian* leaders (of course anonymous), a unique critique of developments throughout the entire period.

The university allotted a term's study leave in the summer of 1972, spent in the Langdale Valley where all my data was transported and chapters written. Wordsworth recommends the late spring and early summer as the best months for the Lakes. This was very definitely *not* the case of May, June, July that year. The blackest clouds gathered day after day over the Langdale Pikes and Crinkle Crags, with the upper end of the valley more or less permanently suffused in gloom. But this provided ideal conditions for intensive and uninterrupted work and the job was, to all intents and purposes, completed. I dedicated this book to the memory of my mother, Shena D. Simon, who died aged 88 that summer. The author of a centenary history of Manchester's government, she had consistently encouraged my historical work.

Attention returned to current educational concerns with a request from my publisher to update my 1953 book on intelligence testing, with the addition of other recent papers on the topic. The outcome was *Intelligence, Psychology and Education* (1971), sub-titled 'A Marxist Critique'. It included my reply to the British Psychological Society's *Secondary School Selection*, a paper on 'Karl Marx and Education' (delivered at the Manchester University School of Education in 1965), the study of classification and streaming just mentioned, and a full length response to Jensen's 'Intelligence, Race, Class and Education' written in 1970. An epilogue set out my own suggestions about internal comprehensive school organisation as various patterns were now jostling for acceptance. A second, revised edition was commissioned a few years on.

Other related studies during the years up to 1975 included a survey of options open to comprehensive schools in determining grouping procedures in the early years, given the rejection of the classic pattern of prismatic streaming. This was presented to the Eugenics Society as part of a lecture on comprehensive education, 'Internal Structure and Organisation'. I explained that little or no research had yet been done on this matter and pointed to many different principles which might determine grouping (e.g. random sampling, balanced 'mixed ability', friendship grouping or personality grouping). The conference, under the title *Equalities and Inequalities in Education* (1975), reflected the widespread interest in a topic still dominant in the field of education. Also worth mentioning is a symposium masterminded by William Taylor on *Research Perspectives in Education* (1973). Following the still dominant four-discipline syndrome with contributions on the philosophy, sociology, psychology and history of education, this also took in the organisation of educational research in the UK, now burgeoning, and its relation to practice. This enabled a reconsideration and critique of current developments in the history of education which in the United States was extending its brief in creative ways and permitted an evaluation of the role of historical research in promoting understanding.

Important theoretical and practical issues continued to surface in education in the mid 1970s during what became a time of continuous crisis, but my main energies were now deliberately diverted towards primary education. I collaborated in a major, publicly-funded research programme into teaching and learning under new conditions in primary schools. This, known as ORACLE, covered my last five years as a professor of education.

THE BLACK BOX

Although only a small minority of primary schools had deliberately made the transition to unstreaming pupils by the
mid-1960s, it was already clear – to informed opinion – that the
movement would spread, probably with extreme rapidity. The
Forum board in its evidence to Plowden had argued strongly
that research resources should be devoted to the internal structure and organisation of the unstreamed (or 'mixed ability')
class, rather than which system – streamed or unstreamed – was
'better'. Mixed ability teaching was rapidly appearing in schools
but no-one knew what strategies and tactics teachers were using,
nor whether unstreaming advantaged certain pupils and disad-
vantaged others – as streaming had done. Where teachers needed
help, and where we thought research should be directed, was
into the techniques best adapted to gain full value from the new
dispensation.

A major research project was already underway when our
evidence was presented to Plowden – that is, the Barker Lunn
NFER initiative. Although established by Boyle in 1963, NFER
did not report until 1970, three years *after* the Plowden report
appeared! Sticking to its brief, the Barker Lunn research sought
to identify 'the one best system'. But the evidence offered was
ambiguous; in essence the report indicated that, in terms of
pupils' learning gains, both systems had generally equivalent
outcomes. Unstreaming, however, did appear to enhance social
gains in comparison with streaming. The Plowden Committee
had already come down unequivocally on the side of non-
streaming. But their report failed to consider the question of
how to teach the unstreamed class, or make any suggestions as to
the pedagogical techniques that might best be adopted. Nor was
there any recommendation that the unstreamed class be a focus
of research.

All this had been going on in the 1960s; the swing to non-
streaming had since intensified so that, by the early 1970s it was
almost impossible to find a streamed primary school in the
country. What then was happening in these unstreamed schools?

What forms of organisation and pedagogical techniques were being established and how did these compare? On these matters there was no public, or research-based knowledge whatsoever. We were in fact in the midst of a major transformation relating to teaching and learning in primary schools, yet hardly anyone seemed to know anything about it. In these circumstances I felt the need to initiate research myself into this whole, fascinating but still secret, field.

A major problem which immediately presented itself arose from the fact that the research envisaged necessarily involved penetration *within* the classroom, if only to discover what was going on. Very little such research, strange though it may seem, had ever been attempted in this country. During the hegemony of mental testing, a very long period, any such attempt seemed totally unnecessary. The classical pattern of enquiry adopted was simple. A 'control' group and an 'experimental' group (or class) of children were identified. The first followed the given curriculum, the experimental group a modified or new curriculum. Tests were administered at the start and close of programmes, from which relative gains were calculated. Conclusions were drawn from this analysis as to which programme was the more 'successful'. No interest whatever was taken in 'process' – the differences between the activity of the two groups and their teachers while the two programmes were being taught. This was regarded as a 'Black Box', impenetrable by any known techniques. For this reason educational researchers had not developed any techniques to penetrate the primary classroom.

If we were to discover differences in pedagogical, or teaching, techniques, and attempt to relate these to differences in pupils' learning, that Black Box had to be penetrated. We needed to locate any major differences in teachers' organisational and pedagogical techniques – more than that, to discover differences in pupils' activities while being taught; and, in particular, to find out how these teacher-pupil and even pupil-pupil interactions differed – given the nature of the 'informal' Plowden-type class-rooms coming into being. An absolute priority was to discover techniques which would permit a reconstruction of both pupil and teacher activity in the primary classroom.

The complexity of this task, and the degree of variation to be found, was dramatically brought home to me in my 'fly on the wall' role as observer in three different primary schools in Leicester. The three teachers concerned had each found their own solution to the problem of teaching an unstreamed class, each apparently motivated by a different philosophy. Teacher A held an extreme 'liberal' outlook, in this closely resembling the Plowden Committee's standpoint. Each child was seen as unique, subject to his or her own (inner) rate of learning. Teaching was, therefore, totally individualised, the thirty or so children in the class each working individually through a series of carefully constructed work-cards. There was no class teaching and no group work whatever; each child worked on his/her own. As each task, or series of tasks, set was completed, the children brought their workbooks to the teacher for checking. So there developed the long straggle to the teacher's desk one came to recognise as symptomatic of this technique.

Teacher B adopted an exactly opposite procedure, as one who totally rejected pedagogical techniques and theories derived from intelligence testing, believing in the educability of the normal child as an article of faith. In this classroom class teaching was the rule. The teacher attempted to phrase her teaching so as to make it intelligible to all. In this case traditional techniques and skills were transferred into the new situation with little attention to so-called 'ability' differences among the pupils.

Teacher C, however, differed from both of these. In her classroom groups of varying size and composition were formed to carry out cooperatively various tasks. Interaction among members of these groups was encouraged, and problem-solving tasks, carefully thought out, presented for joint solution. Here much emphasis was put on the educative value of the pupil-pupil interactional process, the teacher herself circulating actively between the groups monitoring their activities and results. In this third classroom my observations were necessarily confined to the activities of particular groups and the nature of the inter-actional process within these.

It was apparent that teachers, on their own in the new situa-tion, were likely to develop a variety of techniques based both on experience and on 'philosophic' understanding of children's learning – which could be very complex. It also seemed evident that a teacher's approach or 'style', as we came to define it, would itself have, to some extent at least, a determining effect on children's learning. The challenge facing the researcher was to find some means of reflecting the totality of activity in the class-room and to reduce this, if possible, to meaningful categories allowing for the definition of relationships. This was a tall order – or so it seemed at the time.

Financial support for this kind of educational research was becoming increasingly available. In 1967 the Social Science Research Council was established to fund research in the social sciences. Education was part of its remit, work being guided and controlled by an Education Research Board which vetted appli-cations and distributed funds. Michael Young[2] had been appointed by the then Secretary of State, Crosland, as the first Chair of SSRC. Here was an opportunity to be taken up, and, with help and advice from colleagues, I put in a submission for a research grant, sufficient to fund a single research assistant and equipment. The grant materialised and the research was on its way.

My research assistant, Deanne Bealing (later Boydell) – with a good degree in psychology at Leicester and unusually interested in education – proved a researcher of outstanding ability. Given a number of administrative responsibilities within the School of Education I could not undertake active research – hence the application for an assistant. But throughout the five years we worked together (1970-75), my assistant carried through, in an exemplary manner, three sequential projects involving close systematic observation of a number of primary classrooms. We met constantly to discuss procedures and outcomes.

The major problem we faced was to find, or develop, an appropriate instrument for recording both pupil and teacher activities in the classroom. Experiments with radio microphones and other such techniques proved unsuccessful (normally because of an excess of ambient noise). The SSRC encouraged a visit to the USA in order to assess relevant research techniques there; and Deanne made the journey. It was here that the solution to our problem was found. The best known instruments available in the United States mostly assumed a class teaching set-up, and total teacher dominance. These were of no use in the informal primary classroom. However, one American professor had developed an instrument which, with modification, might serve to meet the situation in classrooms characterised by talk and movement among pupils. This was the Pupil Record of School Experience (PROSE). The instrument had been specifically developed in the United States to monitor the 'British' variant of primary school practice incorporated in the Headstart programme. An observer focused on a pre-chosen sample of pupils (say five or six in turn), then on the teacher, and so back. In the event we found it necessary to develop a second instrument – the Teacher Record – in order to pick up sufficient data on the teacher's activities for analysis, our observers using each of the instruments in turn. In this way a reasonably comprehensive set of data could be accumulated recording both teacher and pupil activities, their mobility, interaction, subject studied and so on.

Through a series of intensive trials Deanne modified both instruments, adapting them to the 'informal' primary classrooms which clearly predominated in maintained schools. A detailed manual and handbook was produced for training observers on each of the two instruments. Other techniques for accumulating information were also developed, but the two observational instruments remained central. Once these were adapted and refined we felt ready to launch an effective research study.

I did not consider myself an educational 'researcher' in this area. While the critique of intelligence testing had involved me in the research world of the late 1950s, this was as antagonist rather than participant; reviews by psychologists of my work at that time had been extremely hostile. This situation had changed and there was now an increasing demand for studies of 'process', which necessitated study conducted inside the classroom. In 1970 research specialists David Hamilton (a close friend) and Malcolm Parlett launched a devastating assault on what they called the 'agricultural syndrome', and pressed for anthropologically based 'case study' techniques as best adapted to illuminate the real factors influencing educational procedures.

By 1976 I found myself the President of the new British Education Research Association (launched in 1973). I was also surprised one morning in 1974 by a long-distance call from the Chair of the Education Research Board of the SSRC, encouraging me to submit a proposal for a 'programme' (rather than simply the suggested 'project') of research. A programme could be long term, and should incorporate a design comprising a set of interlocking projects. The suggestion was that a submission for a five year programme, including provision for adequate research assistance and equipment might receive favourable consideration.

ORACLE

As it happened a colleague at the Leicester School of Education, Maurice Galton, was just completing a study of teaching which involved a degree of classroom observation – in this case of secondary school chemistry lessons. Similar problems in our different fields had already been tossed around between us and Maurice and been particularly helpful, especially in the area of statistical analysis. Another very lively member of the school's staff, Jim Eggleston, who had master-minded the science project Maurice worked on (as a research assistant), also proved unfailingly helpful, encouraging and innovative in his thinking. So the nucleus of a research team was already there and the school's concerns began, for the first time, to tilt in the direction of research.

The net outcome of all this was that Maurice and I decided to team up together and plan a serious programme of research into primary school classroom activities – both teaching and learning. We were able quickly to accumulate an impressive team of experienced researchers at Leicester to work with us on the inter-connected projects we were designing. This team included Pat Ashton, who had recently made her name nationally with a report on an intensive research project on primary teachers' aims;[3] it employed a questionnaire technique but focused on a topic clearly relevant to our interests. Also drawn in was Sara Delamont, an ebullient and productive sociologist with research experience in her own field, particularly to study problems of school to school transfer.

The design of the submission was extremely complicated and took a great deal of concentrated labour. We had to explicate precisely how the various inter-related projects would be carried through, what research techniques would be used at each stage, the personnel required and their rates of pay and also equipment. The final document ran to 15,000 words, not one of which (I hope) was wasted. In composing it Deanne and I were fortunate to have two or three productive sessions with the late Professor Jack Tizard, a very experienced educational researcher (recently Chair of the Education Research Board) and a social psychologist of note, the late Hilde Himmelweit, always very helpful and a lovely person. The submission was completed on time.

Our proposal was for a five year programme with three full-time research assistants, together with funds for up to a dozen part-time classroom observers. The first year would be spent setting up the research, contacting schools, gaining first the backing of headteachers and then the cooperation of class teachers. There would follow three years of intensive classroom observation of a sample of classes in three local authority areas – Northampton, Leicester and Sheffield: the data gathering years. The fifth and final year was set aside for analysing the data and writing up results. We were determined that these should be presented as soon as possible and in a form comprehensible to teachers and others interested, since so much research has remained inaccessible due to its jargon-ridden and complex presentation. To glance ahead for moment – we did succeed in this, producing five volumes, published by Routledge. The first was *Inside the Primary Classroom* (1980), the fourth, on transfer studies, *Moving up from the Primary Classroom* (1983), the fifth and final one, *Inside the Secondary Classroom*, in 1986.

The funds requested totalled £86,000 (though, with inflation, the final cost was greater). The four inter-related projects were, first and most important, a study of the relative 'effectiveness' of different teaching approaches in terms of pupils' learning; second, a detailed observational study of the process of pupil transfer to the next stage of their education under different 'systems' (at the ages of nine, ten and eleven); third, the development of new forms of teacher-based assessment appropriate for modern educational approaches; fourth, an examination of the consistency of teaching methods over time.

The central thrust was to define differences in pupil learning and teacher styles respectively, to relate the latter to pupil learning as measured by tests in mathematics, English and reading; and generally to reconstruct both teacher and pupil activity within the classroom and submit it to analysis. The transfer studies and the later study of secondary education had a similar pattern, but relied more heavily on anthropological (case study) data.

The SSRC presumably now began to mull over our submission – that is, to send it to selected experts for comment – so no information was initially available as to how it was received. The crunch came when a high-powered team arrived at Leicester for a full afternoon's session with the team we had recruited. A sharp interrogation followed, particularly close questioning on relevant statistical techniques (e.g. cluster analysis), putting Maurice under pressure. It was an aspect I was glad to leave to another, having no claims to expertise. Maurice emerged with flying colours. All our team participated effectively – in fact we knew precisely *what* we wanted to do, and, thanks to the earlier projects Deanne and I had completed, *how* we were going to do it. The SSRC visitors departed in an amicable atmosphere and a few days later came official confirmation that the submission was approved, together with the funds specified. We were on our way.

The programme proper began in October 1975. Planned for five years, it would finish in October 1980 – precisely the point when, aged 65, I would retire from the university having reached maximum retirement age. So seeing this job through (with Maurice) would see me out, though it was by no means my only responsibility or area of activity during these years; for one thing, from 1974 to 1977 I served my second stint as Director of the School of Education.

To appoint the three research staff who would work full-time on the project was the initial step in implementing our programme. For the senior job we recruited John Willcocks, senior psychologist for Oxfordshire with experience in primary education. For the second an experienced statistician and computer analyst with research experience was needed and we were fortunate to recruit Paul Croll, already involved in research in the area of Mass Communications – a research department at Leicester. For the junior post we needed someone who could train our observers in the use of the two instruments, and develop new forms of assessment for measuring pupils' progress. Deanne had just begun a family and so could not be considered – a sad blow for us, if not for her. She was retained as a consultant and in her place we recruited Anne Jasman, a higher degree student. Jasman had recently trained at Leicester to teach and had herself undertaken an observational research project at Countesthorpe, a local secondary school.

We were fortunate in retaining this central team throughout the five year period. All the three appointed went on to further research and employment in teacher education, Paul Croll being later appointed Professor and Head of Department at Bristol Polytechnic (now the University of the West of England) and then at Reading University. During the year we recruited up to a dozen part-time assistants, who, together with the research staff, would undertake the intensive classroom observation planned for three years. We were lucky again to attract a group of first class people, mostly over qualified women sometimes with small children, looking for flexibly organised part-time work. All were systematically trained by Anne Jasman during the first year in the use of the two key instruments and other data gathering techniques – and all became extremely proficient. Several combined observational work with study for a higher degree on a topic related to the programme (e.g. group work in the primary classroom) for which Maurice and I acted as supervisors. Several of our observers moved on to careers in teacher education in universities and colleges. Meanwhile the ORACLE study generated a powerhouse of research at Leicester, a stimulating experience. The acronym incidentally – a sufficiently striking one – thought up by our research team stands for 'Observational Research and Classroom Learning Evaluation'.

IN THE FIELD

To assemble the staff and the money was a beginning but of course we also needed schools, classrooms and teachers willing to be observed. A representative sample of schools was a requirement and we approached the chief education officers of Northamptonshire, Leicestershire and Sheffield for permission to contact local schools; a mix of urban, suburban, and if possible, some rural schools. The planned inter-related projects meant also identification of the groups of primary schools feeding specific middle or secondary schools. With schools identified in the three areas, the next task was to persuade heads (of secondary and middle as well as primary schools) to allow our observers into specific classes (which we could identify according to our research design) in their schools. This crucial negotiation was undertaken mainly by Maurice, John Willcocks and myself, and generally met with success; we were left to find teachers in their schools prepared to welcome our observers. Normally we could identify precisely which classes in each school we wished to observe in Year One, with a view to following these into a second and sometimes third year.

To our relief subsequent meetings, often with the entire staff of a targeted school, proved fruitful and we were able to carry out the research programme as planned. Individual teachers would gain nothing of significance in participating in the research except the extra strain of accepting an adult observer at their lessons. The fact that the great majority willingly agreed and accepted this situation as their contribution to gaining the knowledge required was, in our view, extremely praiseworthy and indicated clearly the openness of their views and outlook. They were as keen as us to see a scientific analysis of classroom interaction.

When our project was under way, an increasing brouhaha, led by the media, exploded over the issue of the nature of primary education as a whole. I well recall the newspaper and TV reaction to Neville Bennett's *Teaching Styles and Pupil Progress* (1976). This research seemed to indicate that so-called 'formal' teaching was more effective than Plowden-type 'progressivism'. Many primary teachers were shattered by the brutality of much of this publicity, as we discovered on entering schools to win cooperation for our research. Bennett had used a questionnaire method, not classroom observation, and I think ORACLE gained support precisely because teachers recognised that classroom-based research was more likely to provide a true reflection of the situation than one derived primarily from replies to questionnaires.

Another much publicised event at that time was the 'Tyndale case', to the fore for almost a year. A London primary school attracted attention by imposing an extreme version of 'progressivism' which appeared to reduce the school to a state of anarchy. The culmination was a public semi-judicial hearing during which many of the issues at stake were ventilated. As we systematically pursued our research, explosions off seemed increasingly to dominate – *The Times* was devoting leaders to 'the wild men of the classroom'. James Callaghan's now noted speech at Ruskin College, Oxford in November 1976 ventilated the problems of what he called 'modern methods' at Prime Ministerial level. A 'great debate' ensued, and the publication of a polemical 'Black Paper' (March 1977) incorporating a dozen different attacks on 'informal' teaching approaches in primary schools. There was never a greater need for a sober, research-based appraisal as to what exactly was going on in primary school classrooms.

What did we find? I will try to summarise the main findings relevant to contemporary controversy and those of most significance. Some findings detailed in our first publication, *Inside the Primary Classroom* (1980), may be singled out.

We found no evidence to support the widely propagated view that most primary school classrooms were in a state of anarchy – that pupils wasted an inordinate amount of time in talk, play and general rumbustuousness. What chiefly characterised primary classrooms, we found, was a high level of pupil involvement in their tasks. On average pupils were 'fully involved and cooperating on task' (a category in the pupil record) for 58 per cent of their lesson times, involved in 'routine activities' related to their task for 12 per cent of that time, and 'waiting for teacher' for help in or assessment of their work for 5 per cent of the time. This meant that pupils were typically involved in working on their tasks for 75 per cent of lesson time. This is a high level of involvement, probably considerably exceeding what most adults in full-time occupations achieve.

In my view the most significant finding that ORACLE brought to light was what we called the 'asymmetry of teacher-pupil interaction'. It turned out that the great bulk of the 58 classrooms studied were 'informally' organised – normally children were seated in groups rather than rows, though, as we discovered, each child normally worked individually on his or her own task. Classroom organisation, then, tended to follow Plowden precepts regarding the importance of individualising activity and consequently learning. In this situation we found the teacher was hyperactive, interacting with pupils for 80 per cent of lesson time. The pupils, on the other hand, were generally passive, on average interacting *as individuals* with the teacher for only 2 per cent of lesson time. Admittedly we found, in addition, that pupils as a whole interacted with the teacher when the latter addressed the whole class; but generally such class teaching tended to be of short duration, covering only 12 per cent of lesson time. As for group work, as already mentioned, pupils, though seated in groups, tended to work individually. Collaborative group work was rare (10 per cent of all group work observed). Most pupils did not experience this at all. The peda-gogical implications of these findings, in my view considerable, will be discussed shortly.

Another crucial finding gave cause for concern. The Plowden Committee strongly encouraged the move away from what they saw as old-fashioned didactic forms of class teaching. The emphasis was laid on the creation of situations that would encourage discovery and creativity among pupils, as well as enable educative talk and discussion between the teacher and individual pupil. What we found, however, was that, although classrooms were individualised and class teaching unusual, the teachers' interactions with individual pupils were typically very short and overwhelmingly didactic (telling). On the other hand probing (or what we called 'higher order') questioning by the teacher, aimed at making children think, was maximised in the whole class teaching situation; where individualised or group work was in progress, didacticism was the rule. I will return to this point also.

In the meantime an unexpected conclusion thus surfaced: individualisation, regarded as 'progressive', was accompanied by maximum didacticism on the part of the teacher. Whole class teaching, regarded as a 'traditional' approach, maximises probing questioning on the part of the teacher. Data of this order under-lined that differences of approach to teaching in primary classrooms are a great deal more complex than is recognised under the dichotomy 'progressive/traditional' or 'formal/infor-mal', generally accepted as reflecting reality.

This is not the place to detail ORACLE findings, in any case fully reported in the five volumes. We did make a start in identi-fying differences in teaching style (usually linked with organisational differences), isolating four (or six) main types – these were related to learning differences in pupils. It was not our aim to locate 'the one best system', but to cast light on these differences and probe their effect. This was a classic 'process-product' study in design; the outcomes were fully reported in our second volume *Progress and Performance in the Primary School Classroom* (1980). We also identified four 'pupil types' derived from differences in classroom behaviour – 'attention seekers', 'intermittent workers', 'solitary workers' and 'quiet collaborators'. Finally we identified the characteristics of the most 'successful' teachers in terms of pupil gains. Characteristics defined were as follows: high level of teacher-pupil interaction, use of higher order (probing) questioning and stimulation, effectively organised collaborative group work, provision of regular feedback to pupils, 'non-didacticism' (that is avoidance of the tendency continually to instruct children as to how to carry out set tasks), encouragement to children to work by themselves in solving problems, and a tendency towards a broad curriculum as against focusing narrowly on 'the basics'.

PROBLEMS WITH PLOWDEN

Some of the lessons of ORACLE began to form in my mind as data accumulated, to be subjected to analysis and discussion by the research team. In particular it became increasingly apparent that the Plowden insistence on individualising the teaching/learning process presented teachers with a difficult and complex managerial task. The Plowden Committee actually called for a type of university tutorial discussion between the teacher and individual pupil, ignoring the reality, in a class of thirty, of twenty-nine other pupils clamouring for the same attention. Teachers need, above all, to establish an ordered classroom in which all the children know what they are expected to do and to work quietly at their tasks. This, it seemed to us, was why our sample of teachers generally appeared so highly active, interacting with one pupil after another in short bursts, *and* why their interactions were primarily didactic. In the circumstances this was the style necessitated . Pupils needed guidance and help – this took the form of direction, by the teacher. In short, the individualised classroom offered neither time nor opportunity for the long-term individualised interactions Plowden favoured.

This stress on individualisation, which dominates the theoretical section of the Plowden Report, is based on the conviction that each child must be seen as unique, a product of genetic endowment on the one hand, and what was seen as the differentiating process of social interaction as the child matured, on the other. Far from being similar, therefore, children differ uniquely in rate of development over different parameters (intellectual, social, moral). The teacher's task is to 'match' teaching to each individual's unique characteristics, which must be carefully monitored. The Plowden report stressed that all good teaching should be individualised. Hence Plowden's down-grading of whole class teaching and also (another clear weakness) cooperative group work – hardly even considered by the committee.

The problems of such individualisation in teaching are apparent from ORACLE's data. It was increasingly borne in on me that a focus on individualisation actually destroys any possibility of developing effective pedagogical means relevant to the teaching of young children as a whole. The real need, it seemed, was to discover characteristics affecting learning that were common to all children, and so to develop effective pedagogic means relevant to *all*. Total individualisation excluded, even denied, that possibility, while itself providing no clue as to how best to teach a class of thirty children. Indeed it could be a recipe for disaster.

As ORACLE drew to a close I formulated this view in a chapter for a book I edited with William Taylor, *Education in the Eighties*, under the heading 'Why no Pedagogy in England?'. This attempted an historical analysis as to why, in England, pedagogy, 'the science of teaching', had suffered consistent neglect and marginalisation. This ended with a critique of 'Plowden individualisation' and suggestions for a change. Particular attention was drawn to the work of Vygotski in formulating a theoretical basis for a positive approach to pedagogy within the primary school.

Primary education continues to have a high profile, particularly because succeeding Tory secretaries of state continued to use it as a whipping boy – quite evidently for political reasons.

Past ministers, for instance Kenneth Clarke and John Patten, appear to have had a nostalgic desire for a return to yesterday – to an ideal of the primary classroom with rows of well disciplined, silent children subject to didactic mass teaching of the order observed in the 1940s; classes of necessity streamed according to some criterion. This image has been put across in all sorts of way – through press conferences and attributed or non-attributed press briefings retailed by tabloid 'education correspondents'. In the 1990s there has been a recrudescence and around Christmas 1992 Clarke, then secretary of state, appointed a group (dubbed 'the Three Wise Men') to report on teaching and learning in the primary school. This report, mainly by Robin Alexander, drew on the ORACLE findings and more recent research (including his own) to make incisive criticisms of contemporary practice, while also emphasising positive features. The report again insisted that individualisation could not provide a basis for the development of effective forms of teaching and organisation – that the present requirement is for an emphasis on what children have in common as the base from which to operate and clarify a theoretical stance. The imposition of a national curriculum, embodying the definition of common objectives for all children, whatever the criticisms that can be made of its structure and character, does create a new situation and there has been room to discuss the fundamental problems in relation to this modification of practice.[4]

Primary education, so long neglected and still the Cinderella of the education service, is of the utmost importance, and it was a privilege to be closely involved in the work as a researcher and reporter. For a full decade, from 1970 to 1980, I had the opportunity of working with a fine team which met all obligations. My research assistant for five years during the run-up to ORACLE, Deanne Boydell, became head of the Education Department at Westminster College, Oxford; Maurice Galton who partnered me as co-director of the ORACLE project, has been Professor of Education at Leicester for many years and Director of the School of Education. All members of the full-time research team were fully engaged in a cooperative enterprise, while the talented team of part-time observers undertook an arduous programme of observation in an exemplary manner. Through their continuing influence in present employment – and articles in the educational press, innumerable lectures and conferences with teachers up and down the country – the ORACLE message has gradually permeated the educational scene.

ORACLE was undertaken because of its overriding intrinsic interest and bearing on current controversies but it was good to receive the SSRC response to our final report, recognition of 'a most impressive research programme'. Despite the 'very ambitious nature of the research', the team had kept very close to 'the original schedule'; and an 'important and comprehensive series of publications' had emerged to ensure 'effective dissemination'.[5] Assistance for further research into primary education was offered to Maurice Galton who has since carried through a whole series of research projects into primary education, establishing Leicester University as one of the country's leading centres of such studies.

This was one, very welcome, side of the question in the mid-1970s. The other, less welcome, issue was the sudden emergence of a widely publicised blast of criticism directed against educationists and particularly teachers. The root cause of the problems faced by schools has too often been economic; too low a level of expenditure on both equipment and personnel, with which a fine body of teachers, in the main, have had to contend. Nevertheless, should difficulties emerge, the duties and performance of teachers are all too soon under heavy attack. When the political left joined with the detractors of education as a force for human and social benefit, a nadir was reached. Not only were teachers incompetent, the public was told, the school was no tool for human and social betterment: accumulated knowledge was a mere bourgeois construct to be rejected rather than sought. Elected local authorities were the next target for politicians – they should be forced out of action by central direction, their functions taken over by nominated 'quangos' selected by politicians in London. I discussed some of these issues in a series of articles and lectures at this time – including the annual Marx

Memorial Lecture for 1977.

This was particularly apposite at that moment. It may come as a surprise to many that Marx was a strong supporter of local democratic control of education and an equally strong opponent of state control over its content and form. At a moment when precisely this shift was taking place in England, Marx's warnings seemed particularly relevant. Equally, Marx stood for making available to all the knowledge and culture gained by humanity in its climb from savagery to civilisation. He would have had no truck whatsoever with relativist views now making an impact particularly in London schools. Nor would he have sympathised with neo-Marxist and other views that education itself could make 'no difference'; on the contrary he saw a full, all-round education, including technology, as the means of betterment both of individual and social life. And certainly he would have rejected way-out libertarian ideas at that time popular in some circles.

It seemed particularly important at this time to clarify the nature and role of conflicts in education historically and so contribute towards setting the continuous struggle for educational advance on a firm theoretical foundation. Hence the appeal to the authority of Marx then, of course, widely respected among the left. Time off was taken from ORACLE and the Leicester School of Education to attend to these wider questions at a time of sharpening crisis. These ominous developments were taking place, it should be remembered, under a *Labour* government.

The election of May 1979 brought the Tories back in power, with Margaret Thatcher, our old enemy in education, as Prime Minister. This created a new situation nationally. But for me, personally, 1980 also marked a turning point. I had reached retiring age (65) in March that year. In September I cleared my room at the university and prepared for 'retirement'. But much remained to be done. It was not my intention to cultivate my garden.

NOTES

1. Personal communication from Clyde Chitty.
2. Later Lord Young of Dartington, and not to be confused with Michael F.D.Young, mentioned above.
3. P. Ashton, P. Kreen, F. Davies, and B.J. Holley, *The Aims of Primary Education: a study of teachers' opinions*, 1975.
4. Brian Simon, 'Some Problems of Pedagogy, Revisited', reprinted in *The State and Educational Change: Essays in the History of Education and Pedagogy*, London 1994, pp 147-61.
5. Our main book, *Inside the Primary Classroom*, sold well over 10,000 copies; *Progress and Performance* nearly 5000. Total sales of all five books exceeded 20,000.

8

'Retirement', 1980-1997

For seventeen years I watched from the sidelines an uninterrupted period of Tory rule; a sustained effort to reverse the
achievements of the 1960s and 1970s. This naturally set the
agenda – the need to combat the worst excesses of educational
policy under Thatcher and her successor. On the other hand,
now without regular full-time employment – in teaching, editing, administration and research – new scope was available for
thinking and writing; also for travel to experience more about
twentieth century education further afield.

Travel abroad

Early in 1981 I spent a semester at the University of Melbourne
as 'Fink' lecturer, to take courses and deliver the annual Fink
lecture. While there I was also able to lecture and lead seminars
at Sydney, Canberra, Newcastle and Armidale. At Melbourne I
was looked after by old friends, travelling I made new. My next
port of call was Canada, to report on ORACLE with Maurice
Galton at crowded meetings of the Canadian Educational
Association held at Halifax. This was followed by a second visit
in 1983, this time to Vancouver where my wife and I were jointly
appointed 'Green' visiting scholars at the University of British
Columbia (UBC) to lecture on the history of education and
intelligence testing. Here we spent several late-summer weeks
accommodated palatially in the staff club overlooking the ocean,
having reached Vancouver by the spectacular Canadian Pacific

Railway route across the prairies and through the Rocky Mountains – a journey now no longer possible. We also visited Victoria University and stopped off at Toronto on the way home for seminars at the Ontario Institute for the Study of Education. At Vancouver we received greetings from Cecil and Ida Green, benefactors of many different facilities in Canada and elsewhere, including Green College at Oxford. A Vancouver graduate student, indeed UBC's first Indian Ph.D., invited us to his Indian reserve where we feasted on the traditional salmon. While at Vancouver we participated in a joint conference of the Canadian and American History of Education Societies – a stimulating occasion and the chief reason for the timing of our visit.

In 1980 the International Society for the Study of the History of Education (ISCHE) was established, covering Europe as a whole (both East and West) of which I became the first president. This certainly broadened my experience, particularly through annual conferences held in many centres: Louvain (now Leuven), Paris, Oslo, Warsaw, Budapest, Wolfenbüttel with its famous library, Salamanca, Parma, and Zürich. This organisation did much to extend the outlook of the English beyond peculiar local concerns, whose intricacy too often absorbed us. Even visits to Ireland and Scotland contributed in this way. The most important link was that between Eastern and Western Europe, maintained during the cold war. Remarkably, given the problems of current life in Moscow, the most recent international publication was edited there by Olga Salimova – the same who came to my aid as translator and assistant on my first visit to meet psychologists and educationists in the Soviet Union in 1955. A woman of great courage and commitment, she has an unquenchable vision of the key importance of education and was determined, come what may, to inspire a new generation with the importance of education, its study and history. The book in question, *Why Should We Teach History of Education?* concerned with the objectives of history of education in teacher training, contributed to by leading historians from many nations has recently been reprinted due to increasing demand in Russia and other European countries.

While work has often taken me around Europe, my only recent visit to the United States was to a symposium at Harvard in 1994 organised by the National Academy of Education of the United States, after election as a 'Foreign Associate Emeritus' member. This offered a welcome opportunity for talk with Jerome Bruner about the work of Alexander Luria and of his own popularisation of Vygotski's work in the United States. My wife and I also attended a meeting of the National Academy held at Stockholm – the Americans have close academic links with the Swedes – and here I especially enjoyed meeting with Thorsten Husen, who chaired many of the sessions. Of almost exactly my age, Husen master-minded the Swedish transition to comprehensive education from the late 1940s, playing a leading role in the many research projects involved. He is certainly the 'grand old man' of the Swedish reform.

My main adventure abroad, however, was back in 1984, when I travelled to Japan. I spent a month in Tokyo looked after by a trio of friends dubbed 'The Three Musketeers' – Professors Horio, Maseo Ota and Fujioka, all fluent in English and familiar with Britain and its educational problems. Appearances to lecture at Japanese universities were formal occasions – at Sendai, Kyoto, Nagoya, Hiroshima and of course Tokyo – but one was received with warmth, even affection. My historical series and other books have been translated into Japanese, and many Japanese scholars have visited Leicester over the years, several studying there for a term or year. The most memorable lecture and reception, however, was at Chuo University near Tokyo, a university then celebrating its centenary. It had been established by a group of admirers of English law and still retained sentiments associated with that origin. I had been asked for a specially prepared lecture on 'The Middle Temple One Hundred Years Ago', the institution where the founder had studied in the 1880s. Enquiry into the subject, with the help of legal friends, was both a recreation and informative for me. The university's reception of the lecture was memorable. During this visit I also gave a special set of six lectures on contemporary educational issues in England, to be translated and published together with papers by Horio, then professor of education at the leading Tokyo university, as a book, *Educational Reform in England and Japan* (1987). Since Japan has a comprehensive system of education at least to 16, many issues of importance are similar in both countries.

Another international experience during these years was participation in a cross-national socio-historical project covering the period 1860-1920. The initiative came from Detlef Müller, a dynamic professor at the new University of Bochum in the Ruhr (Westphalia), after the university had won generous funding for a comparative study of cultural developments in Western Europe in the nineteenth and twentieth centuries. The outcome was a volume entitled *The Rise of the Modern Education System: Structural Change and Social Reproduction, 1870-1920*, edited by Detlef Müller, Fritz Ringer and Brian Simon – published jointly by the Cambridge University Press and Maison des Sciences de L'Homme (1987). The study covered developments in Germany, France and England.

My first task was to recruit a team of English historians of education and I was fortunate in getting a group very well able to interpret English educational reconstruction during the period – Hilary Steedman, David Reeder, John Honey, Roy Lowe. All attended well-organised and intensive seminars at Bochum, together with German, American and French co-workers. For the final volume I took the opportunity to revise aspects of the interpretation in my initial volume of historical studies, published over twenty years earlier (in 1960). More generally certain themes (Müller's 'systematisation' theory, Ringer's 'segmentation') aided explication of patterns of development in secondary education common to all three countries. Fritz Ringer is an American historian of German origin, with an expert knowledge of French developments. The team was well-qualified to tackle the crucial issue – how it was that the generally inchoate structures of the early ninteenth century were, in all three countries, transformed into 'hierarchical and structured systems' with interesting similarities and differences in development.

The collective work with historians of education from America and Germany was a new and much appreciated experience. My paternal grandfather derived from Germany and thereby hangs a tale. Born in 1835 in Breslau he was brought up in boyhood by his uncle, Heinrich Simon, a leading member of the 1848 Frankfurt parliament forced to flee to Switzerland when this was forcibly dispersed in May 1849. He had taken with him the official Seal of this historic parliament, the springboard of democratic development in modern Germany; my grandfather, who came to England in 1860, preserved it and in his turn my father and so it had passed on to my brother and me. On the occasion of my last visit to Bochum, after publication of the book, an honorary degree was conferred on the President of the Bundestag, Frau Dr. Süssmuth, at a moment when the unification of East and West Germany was in train (1990). My family decided this was an appropriate moment to return the historic Seal to its proper place in the Bundestag by way of presentation to the President. She received it with emotion and a promise that a place would be found in the new building planned in Berlin. It was a moving occasion. There was another ceremony too relating to this connection, at the impressive Heinrich Simon monument at Murg in Switzerland, erected to his memory by friends and colleagues after he had drowned in the lake there in 1860. This time the speaker, on an anniversary occasion, was the mayor of the small town which has sedulously cared down the years for a monument erected by supporters of the Frankfurt Parliament – a message also coming from Dr. Süssmuth sending support. By contrast, I have learnt that the story of this Parliament's policy and outlook has yet to be effectively incorporated in the history taught to German children, as against celebrating Bismarck.

HISTORICAL STUDIES

Completion of research and studies for the Bochum volume (published 1987) enabled my return to a long-planned project:

finalising the three volume series on the history of English education by addition of a further volume bringing the analysis up to date. The last study, of the inter-war period, had been published in 1974, concluding around 1939 though with a glance at the future. The new study, then, was planned to cover from 1940 through to the present day taking in the Tory government's 1988 Education Act which very clearly created a new situation. Entitled *Education and the Social Order, 1940-1990*, the 1000 pages of manuscript was finally handed over to my publishers at the beginning of January 1990. As this included many complicated tables of statistics (which took several months to complete) passage through the press was a lengthy business. But to complete it in 1991, ending with a preliminary assessment of the 1988 Act, gave a certain satisfaction.

This study gave the opportunity for a re-assessment of the 1944 Education Act, by now variously evaluated by historians (and politicians). What I define as 'the democratic programme', pressed by reformers during the war, and including integration of the 'public schools' within a locally controlled democratic system – which had gained wide support – had been effectively side-tracked by the then President of the Board of Education, R.A. Butler. Other progressive features, for instance overcoming the so-called 'dual system' whereby voluntary schools co-existed with local maintained schools, had also been successfully held at bay. While important gains, particularly recognition of 'secondary education for all' were achieved, overall the opportunity for a radical reform had been missed. One outcome, of course, was the long drawn out struggle in succeeding years to overcome the divided system now imposed, by Labour as well as Tory governments. However, at that time, this was an issue for the future.

One thing that I was determined on was to accord full credit to the 1960s as a key period for educational advance across the board – at primary, secondary and higher stages. Actually the halcyon years were 1958 to 1972, preceded by a difficult post-war period and succeeded by the Thatcher years and their outcome through to the late 1990s. One feature of this period was an ideological offensive from the right wing intent on rubbishing educational advances of the 1960s on all counts, pointing to these as the cause of present discontents – a distortion of reality. No doubt there were certain excesses, but the period was one of high hopes (in education), optimism and recognisable educational improvement. The time had come to evaluate this process of change and place it in perspective. Three lengthy chapters were devoted to this period, on higher, secondary and primary education respectively. It was good that the book was singled out for welcome in 1991 both by the History of Education Society and the Standing Conference for Studies in Education which unites scholars from all disciplines bearing on education.

There was also another long-standing project to complete. That was to fill out the picture of English developments by focusing on the labour movement's involvement in adult education in the early years of this century – a matter which demanded re-assessment as new material became available. This was attempted in a symposium I now edited, published as *The Search for Enlightenment: the Working Class and Adult Education in the Twentieth Century* in 1990. My introductory chapter ('The Struggle for Hegemony, 1920-1926') traces inter-relations, particularly early conflicts between the Workers' Educational Association and the National Council of Labour Colleges as a background for papers carrying the story through to the modern age; a task lightened by publication of two books by leaders of the movement for 'Independent Working Class Education' (or IWCE, as it was known), both of whom I had got to know in their old age – W.W.Craik, Principal of the Labour College and J.P.M. (Jim) Millar, long-time Secretary of the NCLC whose *The Labour College Movement* appeared in 1979. Bringing the story up to date was made possible by a contribution of three brilliant chapters by an expert in developments in trade union education from 1945, John McIlroy. Two old friends contributed original work, Edmund and Ruth Frow whose remarkable library accumulated over many years now forms the Working Class Library at Salford. The foreword came from the trade union leader, Jack

Jones, himself a product of IWCE, while a closing chapter by Bob Fryer set a future agenda for working class education. A paperback edition was issued by the National Institute of Adult and Continuing Education. There is a note in my diary, written when preparing this volume along with my own historical study, which included many complex tables: 'I have never worked so intensively in my life'.

In all, in seventeen years from 1980, besides editing or writing several books, I produced, or responded to requests for some sixty articles on a wide variety of topics. I used the opportunities offered to enable me to sort out my own ideas on the nature of the relationship between educational and social change, finding myself instinctively in opposition to what became a fashionable view, embraced by both left and right, in the 1970s which presented education as helplessly determined by existing social and economic circumstances. I wished to enhance the view that the process of education itself, through transforming its subjects, could contribute, and has contributed spectacularly, to social change, if in the long rather than the short run. It was this view that I sought to express in various contexts during these years. 'Can Education Change Society?', for instance, was the title of the main lecture delivered at the University of British Columbia during our visit there. This concluded that contemporary interpretations ignored human subjective experience – people's capacity for movement, for acting on the environment, transforming it and so creating a new situation. The future, I concluded, is undecided. Those involved in education should recognise this, and struggle consistently to recognise, and exploit, its potential.

Another opportunity lay in the Fink Lecture at Melbourne, already mentioned, entitled 'Education in Theory, Schooling in Practice: the Experience of the last Hundred Years'. This focused more specifically on the striking contrast between the generally optimistic outlook of the period 1880-1900 compared with the stagnation and fatalism which dominated during the inter-war years. In both cases there was a close link between the dominant theoretical outlook as to the potentialities of education (and so of human beings) – optimistic at the close of the nineteenth century, strongly pessimistic (with the rise of mental testing) in the 1920s and 1930s. I focused here on the contemporary need once again to unite theory and practice but now on a new level 'to the advantage of human development and social change'.

An opportunity to challenge sociological determinism in the interpretation of education arose with the invitation to deliver the annual Charles Carter lecture at Lancaster in 1990. The topic had to be in the field of higher education and my mind went back to my involvement in the student movement of the 1930s. The lecture, under the title 'The Universities and Social Change', used the example of two earlier movements among university students and staff which sought to make a significant impact on society at large – that focused at Cambridge in the early 1790s (in which Samuel Taylor Coleridge played a part) and that at Oxford in the 1880s, strongly influenced by T.H. Green. Both of these movements, I argued – the first hidden from history until quite recently – had a considerable impact on social and political developments generally. Educational institutions, under certain circumstances and even, perhaps, in spite of themselves, had certainly brought about significant change in society at large. There is no reason why they should not do so in the future.

The Lancaster lecture relates to two other initiatives on related themes. I had for long been fascinated by Coleridge's transition, at the turn of the century, from the radical 'Enlightenment' philosophic materialism he espoused so whole-heartedly in his youth to an equally whole-hearted embrace of contemporary German Idealism. Here was another aspect of the battle against determinism as fought by Coleridge himself in his transition from a philosophic standpoint that accepts the individual child's total determination by social or psychological factors (as presented by a mechanistic form of associationism) to one which accepted the power of human beings to appropriate knowledge and 'reproduce it in fruits of his own'; in other words to engage in creative activity. I was struck here with the parallel between Coleridge's intellectual development and that experienced by Karl Marx some decades later when, in his Theses on

Feuerbach, he also recognised the value of idealist thinking in clarifying the dynamic relationship between the individual and the environment. Marx, following Coleridge, sees human subjective activity, or self-change, as the key. I greatly enjoyed this exercise, especially immersion in the astonishing series of volumes comprising the highest levels of scholarship in Coleridge's Collected Works. Much of this essay was written in the Langdale Valley, redolent of Coleridge's and Wordsworth's troubled friendship.

Time was found also to tie up certain loose ends in historical analyses on issues still having a contemporary significance. Chief among these was the process by which the establishment of the top 'public schools' as a system in the mid-late nineteenth century was brought about, involving, as it did, the privatisation of what were, in fact, national assets. The key institution here was Eton College, recently revealed as one of the wealthiest corporate institutions in the country with assets exceeding £130 million. Interest attaches to the parliamentary techniques used to ensure that the outcome of legislation benefited those who stood most to gain from the restructuring of education at this time, in particular the use of Executive Commissioners to cushion reform at this crucial moment. The malign results of all this are still with us in the divided system of education which is one of England's most wounding peculiarities. This, and other essays and lectures bearing on the so-called 'charitable status' of the public schools, their role and function, were collected in a recent publication, *The State and Educational Change: Essays in the History of Education and Pedagogy* (1994). More generally an opportunity to update and restate views on the history of education as an important area of study derived from a series of lectures marking the centenary of Cambridge University's involvement in teacher education (in 1983), master-minded by Paul Hirst, then Professor there. 'Educational Theory and its Foundation Disciplines' was the title of the series, patterned on the model originally introduced in Tibble's *The Study of Education* in 1966, and by now under criticism. But this gave the opportunity to focus again on the historical contribution. With the historian Owen Chadwick as a prestigious and generous chairperson the lecture took place in the Mill Lane lecture room where, some fifty years earlier, I had arranged for Maria Montessori to lecture to our modest Education Society. For me, then, this was a slightly nostalgic experience. Taking the opportunity again to challenge determinist theories I was concerned to emphasise the complexity of the social, political and ideological forces impinging on educational change and the importance of their close analysis for understanding.

A leading concern over this whole period was to underline the scope, and the need, for individual or co-operative action within education – at classroom level, in the school, the region or locality and, not least, on the national scene to bring about desirable change; that is, against supine acceptance of the status quo. In the late 1970s the ORACLE project, together with administrative responsibilities, took much of my time and energy. But in 1978 an opportunity arose to assess the whole direction English education was now taking. Centralised state direction was now on the march. 'Flashpoints of recurring tension', as Maurice Kogan put it, were leading to the politicisation of education on a quite new level – pleas for the substitution of a strong, centralised direction of the whole process were on the increase. Claims were being pressed for central control not only of the structure of the system but over its inner essence – the curriculum, examinations. Now was the time for those critical of such a tendency to make a stand.

The opportunity came with a series of public lectures laid on by the Education Committee, commemorating my mother's work for education in Manchester, given in the Great Hall of Manchester Town Hall in the late 1970s. In 'To Whom Do Schools Belong', given in 1978, I used the title of an historical study by a scholarly chief education officer, W.O. Lester Smith, in which he argued very strongly against increased central control, and in favour of local responsibility and initiatives. Smith's book was published as long ago as 1945, but his theme was still relevant. The strength and vitality of the new forms of local control and initiative that evolved from the late nineteenth century, especially in the North of England, were recalled in this lecture, together with the work and influence of some of the outstanding teachers in those and later years. If we are to retain the characteristic resilience and vitality of our educational system, I argued, what is needed is a *greater* degree of local responsibility for the control of education – 'not curtailment of what we have'. The demand for enhanced central control is often motivated not by considerations related to effective provision to meet social needs but by such criteria as managerial efficiency in the pursuit of economy. There should be due awareness of what may lie behind insistent demands for centralisation, and a readiness to resist moves in what can only be a retrograde direction.

This lecture was given just ten years before Margaret Thatcher launched her devastating assault on local authorities in the 1980s. At least it set on record my own view of the contribution these had made to educational progress and change up to that time.

THE LEGISLATIVE ONSLAUGHT 1988-1997 AND THE RESPONSE

A year after the Manchester lecture, and while I was still in place at Leicester University engaged on the ORACLE project, the first Thatcher government had been returned – in May 1979. Although early indications were given of the line of policy, few would have thought that we were in for nearly eighteen years of Tory rule, driven by increasingly hard-line right-wing policies, aiming to transform what had been a co-operative enterprise into one driven by market forces setting school against school in the struggle for survival. This is not the place to analyse these developments in any detail – that is a matter for future historians and social analysis. While some things needed putting right, the damage done has been incalculable. As I write, the new Labour government, elected on 1 May 1997, is starting work with the aim of writing a new page in the history of national education. This is clearly essential.

Conservative policy immediately following the election victory of 1979 was influenced by the rise of new right pressure groups which had germinated 'like dragon's teeth' over the previous ten or fifteen years. An article contributed to a left progressive journal in 1980 focused on this influence in education as one factor behind the Tory electoral victory – together with weaknesses in Labour policy and actions. The two Bills introduced rapidly by the new government were analysed; one declared that comprehensive education was no longer 'national policy' by repealing Labour's 1976 Act, allowing local authorities to retain existing divided systems and even to reinstate them (none did); the other legitimated a significant shift of public funds from the state to the private sector by establishing the Assisted Places Scheme. This also extended the scope of 'parental choice', opening the way by which 'popular' schools could become middle-class enclaves while inner city schools catering for the working class go to the wall. Here was the beginning of a deliberate polarisation of the school system which became so clear a feature over succeeding years. While clarifying these policies the article was also critical of the left and progressive movement's confusions and ambiguities in educational policy, not only in terms of structure but also in relation to the content, methods, and direction of schooling itself. The left was split on a number of questions, being also strongly infected by libertarian ideas, culpably leaving the defence of 'standards' in education to Rhodes Boyson and the right generally. It seemed at that time, however, that a strong, popular movement in defence of democratic procedures and control could be mounted, and this was called for.

Following this early bout of activity, however, the government, having perhaps other priorities (the trade union movement, local government), relapsed into a strange inactivity while Keith Joseph, Thatcher's 'mentor' took over as Secretary of State for five long years (1981-86). Articles analysing developments over this period focused on the now clearly evident centralising determination of both Minister and Ministry – with the consequent downgrading of local government – together with new tactics following the defeat of the attempt to reintroduce a selective system at Solihull and elsewhere (September

1984). Two years later 'The Battle of the Blackboard' (June 1986) highlighted the desperate search for new populist solutions in education and the internal battles within the Tory party for Joseph's succession. These articles analysed Tory policy as it developed and assessed its implications, attempting also to define a policy around which left-progressive forces could unite to ensure, if possible, the victory of alternative policies.

In May 1987 Keith Joseph finally resigned as Secretary of State to be replaced by Kenneth Baker. The two-year 'teacher action' on salaries, which soured all relationships, had dragged on and on, no solution having been found or even, apparently, thought desirable. But now suddenly the Conservative government decided to 'do something' about education (in Margaret Thatcher's words), and it was indeed essential that something be done if the Tory party was to retain any credibility at all in this area. After various measures, including the handing out of a great deal of pre-election money, a general election in June 1987 once more returned the Tories with a large parliamentary majority. A few days later proposals for radical legislation on education surfaced, to be known, initially, as the Great Education Reform Bill. So-called 'Consultation Papers' were rushed out in midsummer. The Bill itself, it was announced, would be published in November with the objective of its passing through Parliament by the late summer of 1988.

I, and all my friends without exception, saw the projected Bill, as revealed in the Consultation Papers, as a direct threat to comprehensive education, and also to the educational values embodied in that reform. Indeed the encouragement intended to market forces as the main determinant of educational change represented a clear challenge to the principle of co-operative endeavour, mutual solidarity and locally accountable democratic control which we saw as the very keystones of advance. Further, the announcement of what originally appeared as a very crude out-dated national curriculum to be imposed from above, together with mass testing at 7, 11, 14 and 16 seemed, at the time, almost unbelievable. Clever presentation and politics, in the light of almost unanimous protests, softened these latter features over the next few months, but the immediate impact was shocking in the extreme. The early summer of 1987, then, saw widespread protests against almost every feature of the Bill.

It was difficult to react quickly since details of the proposals had been published in a piecemeal manner over the summer – the final 'Red Book', on the curriculum and testing, only appeared late in July. Responses had to be in within two months and the government made it clear that it intended to push its Bill through quickly. I was working on the fourth volume of my historical studies at the time and hoping to complete it shortly. But at the end of July I was asked for an authoritative article on the government's plans by a leading journal. This, entitled, 'Lessons in Elitism', I produced rapidly, covering all the proposals now being put: Local Management of Schools, Open Entry, Grant Maintained Schools and opting out, City Technology Colleges (not actually in the Bill), the National Curriculum and Assessment, attempting to clarify how each of these measures related to the others in what was clearly a right-wing inspired attempt to transform the whole structure, balance and ethos of the educational system, putting particular emphasis on the threat these measures constituted for the continuance of healthy and effective local education authorities. This article, published early in September, was widely disseminated – on a visit to Liverpool shortly after, I found that the Chair of the Education Committee (a university teacher at that time) had circulated copies to his entire committee, while a party of twenty or more Japanese teachers, professors and others who came to see me at Windermere in September were all clutching copies, bought at railway bookstalls.

The annual conference of the British Educational Research Association took place early in September that year at Manchester. Things had happened so quickly that there was no item on the packed agenda relating to the proposed legislation, and yet it would affect everyone there in one way or another. One slot on the programme was available for 'late papers', so, feeling there should be discussion, I offered one on the proposed Education 'Reform' Bill. Expecting a dozen or so to turn up I reconstituted the article mentioned above, already written but not published, for delivery here. I little expected to disrupt the entire conference, but this is what happened – and not because of me, but because of the genuine concern of those present to discuss the issues. Over two hundred turned up. I grabbed my old friend David Hamilton to take the chair and gave the paper to what *The Times Educational Supplement* described as a 'packed meeting'.

My notes record, 'great success'. Obviously this was the one thing all wanted to discuss and appreciated a lead on it. Peter Mortimore (now Director of the Institute of Education London University) said he agreed with 97 per cent of what I said. Jack Wrigley (Professor of Education at Reading University) said he was sure 99 per cent would agree with 99 per cent of what I said (and he was a statistical expert!). On the session finishing a crowd came round the podium holding their hands out like starving children for the paper – fortunately I had brought some copies. In the afternoon at the Annual General Meeting, which I could not attend, the association unanimously adopted the stance defined, deciding to send a letter to Kenneth Baker which was drafted later and dispatched with many signatures.

Earlier that August, before the BERA conference but immediately after publication of the Consultation Papers, Nanette Whitbread, co-editor of Forum, telephoned saying the journal must respond to these and 'give a lead'. Reluctantly agreeing (I was deep in historical studies), a meeting was organised at my house for a group of Editorial Board members, as a result of which our response to each of the papers was drafted, agreed, printed, inserted as extra 'copy' into the September (1987) number of Forum, and then sent to the press, to a substantial proportion of members of both Houses of Parliament, and of course to the Secretary of State (together with thousands of other submissions, all of which were totally ignored). This number of Forum, marking in fact our 30th anniversary, carried a critical early analysis of the proposed Bill which, we held, comprised a set of measures that, related together, could be seen 'as the means of disrupting local systems of comprehensive education'. More detailed analysis was promised for the future.

Towards the end of October that year my publishers, Lawrence and Wishart, phoned me with a proposition to produce an 'instant' book on the forthcoming Bill, to be completed by early December and published in March. After a day or two's thought, I agreed. I had by now a pretty fair idea of the Bill's likely contents, although it was not yet published, and of my attitude to these (largely negative). Also Joan and I were due for a week at Hellsgarth very shortly. The aim was a book of just 40,000 words – space enough both to focus on the main measures the Bill was likely to contain, and our critique of these. In fact the job was done in twenty-four days, though on six of these other things intervened, an average of about 2000 words a day. Mostly I wrote in the mornings, once or twice arising at 5 a.m., relaxed in the afternoons, looked through and prepared material for the next day's spurt in the early evening. As predicted, the Bill, when published in mid-November, contained no variation whatsoever on the plans set out in the preliminary papers – a revealing comment on the nature of this particular 'consultation', as many noted at the time. On the other hand this certainly eased the process of analysis. The MS, corrected and retyped, was finally sent off on time (9 December). *Bending the Rules, the Baker 'Reform' of Education* was published, also as planned, on 16 March 1988. Debates on the Bill had started before Christmas and the Bill was about to start its passage in the Lords where, it was expected, some modifications might be won. The government's majority of over 100 in the Commons ensured an easy passage through that House.

Bending the Rules was launched at a lively press conference in a Fleet Street pub in mid-March attended by two presidents of the National Union of Teachers, several journalists of course, and by Tessa (Lady) Blackstone whose work I greatly respect and who spoke very appreciatively of the book. This sold over 1500 in its first month and had to be reprinted, and revised four times over the rest of 1988 and the next year. This meant that it could be consistently up-dated as new events unfolded. As things worked out, it neither prevented the Bill being passed (!), nor led to any serious modifications. But perhaps it helped to keep alive alternative perspectives and strengthen resistance to specific aspects of the legislation such as opting out. But to evaluate the effectiveness of any piece of literature is notoriously difficult. In any case, I felt I had to do it.

The Forum Editorial Board had decided earlier to give expression to our distaste for Kenneth Baker's Bill by organising a mass 'demonstrative conference', in co-operation with other organisations, against the Bill. Educational associations, teachers' unions, professional organisations, Trade Unions and the Trade Union Congress were all, at this stage, totally opposed to the Bill, and Forum invited these to participate in the organisation of the conference, and to share the cost. This conference took place at Friends' House, Euston Road in London, attracting well over 500 participants from the 26 national organisations taking part. Addressed by Tessa Blackstone, Tim Brighouse (then Oxfordshire's CEO), the late Harry Rée, Michael Armstrong and one representative from each of the 26 participating organisations, this lasted all day and was certainly a resounding success. Edward Blishen kindly wrote the conference report for *Forum* (Vol. 30, No. 1) as he had for our first conference on non-streaming in primary schools some thirty years earlier. Forum Board members acted as stewards controlling what was, once again, even in adversity (or especially so), a team effort. The conference closed with the passage by acclamation of a Statement of Intent, pledging those present 'to continue the fight against this reactionary measure' and, if passed, 'to carry through a powerful campaign to protect schools and colleges from the Bill's worst effects, and to preserve and develop the publicly provided system of education at all levels'. Finally conference pledged itself 'to fight to strengthen the existing system of comprehensive primary and secondary education under popular, democratic control'.

It can be imagined that all this put back progress on what I regarded as my own (historical) work. But when involved in a struggle it is best to give it one's whole energy. Once the Bill was published people naturally wanted to discuss it and define their attitude. Early in December 1987 the Liverpool Education

Committee organised a full day conference for Governing Bodies, teachers' associations, parent groups and others, with some 400 present addressed by Jack Straw (recently appointed Labour spokesman on education) and myself – three months later they ran a second, follow-up conference which I also attended. The level of awareness as to the implications of the Bill was very high. In April 1988 the National Union of Teachers invited me to lecture on 'What Future for Education?' at their annual conference at Scarborough, an enjoyable occasion marked with a high seriousness and quick appreciation of key points. BERA ran perhaps the first conference on the National Curriculum, now looming, at which Richard Pring, Klaus Weddell, Beverley Anderson and I all spoke offering various lines of action but, of course, all critical. Teachers', parents' and Labour movement meetings at Hounslow, Coventry, Oxford, Leeds and Waltham Forest rounded off my personal programme up to the end of August 1988 when the Bill finally received Royal Assent. After that a new chapter opened, with different, if related objectives. A strong battle had been conducted, in the late spring and early summer, by the Labour Party spokespeople in the House of Lords, led by an old friend from my student days, Nora David (née Blakesley). She and Tessa Blackstone, also now a working Labour peer, had been very supportive when I was writing *Bending the Rules* and it was good to observe their very effective debating powers at first hand in the chamber in May. It was good also to see Michael Stewart operating after all these years. Of course Liberal Democrats, cross-benchers and the Anglican bishops in that House all opposed various aspects of the Education Bill. Some of them were extremely knowledge-able in the field of education and they put up an effective fight. There was victory on some issues, as is well known, but the main thrust of the Bill could hardly be deflected in the Upper House. At least it underwent a severe examination.

Once the Bill received Royal Assent, in August 1988, a new situation of course developed, requiring close monitoring and critical assessment. The focuses for such a critique were the main measures in the Act which now began to be implemented. This was maintained consistently over the next few years through Forum which continued to defend local authority responsibility for education and to monitor the early phases of the move towards opting out (Grant Maintained Schools), the continued failure (and farcical nature) of the City Technology College initiative, the impact of the early phases of LMS (Local Management of Schools), and above all, increasingly dramatic developments in the field of the National Curriculum and Assessment. I continued as co-editor of this journal (with Nanette Whitbread) until 1990, when (now aged 75) I finally gave it up, handing over to my friend and ex-student Clyde Chitty who had by now established himself as a foremost critic and historian of the curriculum. This had kept me closely in touch with developments in the schools and among administrators.

I also found myself invited, over the next year or two, to give a number of lectures to various bodies, most of which gave the opportunity for a running critique of the new measures as they unfolded. Almost immediately after the Bill received Royal Assent, in September 1988, the British Education Management and Administration Society requested a lecture, at their annual conference, on a topic clearly congenial to me personally: 'Maintaining Progress Towards a Fully Comprehensive System'. The other keynote lecturer at this conference was to have been Bob Dunn, Schools Minister, but, as he had been sacked by this time, his place was taken by Sir David Hancock, then Permanent Secretary at the DES, who gave government policy the subtle gloss civil servants are so expert at, aiming, presumably, to present it as acceptable to what was largely a local authority and teacher audience (who proved very receptive to my thesis).

Two months later, at the annual conference of the Association of Metropolitan Authorities which then united most of the urban authorities in England and Wales, another keynote speech was given focusing very closely on the opting out and other initiatives which, by now, very clearly threatened the destabilisation of local education authorities generally since it struck at their central responsibility in running school systems. The Chair on this occasion was taken by the Chair of the Manchester

Education Committee (a Councillor from Wythenshawe) who had specifically asked for the job, opening with some kind remarks about both my parents, which I found quite moving. The other 'keynote' speaker at this conference was Angela Rumbold, then a junior Minister who, apparently, had lost the sympathy of her audience by her sharp, flustered and bad-tempered responses to questions (I was not present at her lecture). Here again, it seemed to me, a good spirit was certainly manifest among the delegates the great majority of whom, at that time, represented Labour authorities. They were determined to maintain, and develop their systems of comprehensive education. I got a grass roots 'feel' of the strength of this movement a little later when, in January 1989, the St. Helens local education authority arranged a conference for governors, teachers, parents and councillors on the existing phase of education and their policy. Invited to speak on 'The Future of Comprehensive Education', I found a close solidarity among all of those present in defence of their system and in their strong determination to maintain and strengthen it. No-one, it seemed, was thinking of opting out.

Other opportunities to evaluate the impact of the Act as it began to bite, and perhaps to assess its historical significance in a wider context, came during the next two years (1990-1). The British Education Research Association celebrates the life and thinking of Lawrence Stenhouse, who very sadly died prematurely in 1982, with a lecture at its annual conference. Lawrence had been a close friend and a pioneer in his work on curriculum reform, much revered by all who knew him (particularly teachers). This, then, gave an opportunity not only to recall Lawrence's contribution but also to evaluate the significance and nature of the National Curriculum now being imposed on every maintained school in the country. A month later, I gave a lecture celebrating the Centenary of the establishment of the Department of Education at the University of Newcastle, which allowed a close analysis of the shift to a market economy in education, and of its probable outcomes. This lecture recalled the views of the classical political economists (particularly Adam Smith, Ricardo and

Malthus, but also James Mill and others) and indicated that their teaching on the issue of the finance of education and the market economy bore little relation to the teaching of the so-called Adam Smith Institute, then an increasingly influential right-wing Tory think tank.

This group of analytical, and if I dare say so, critical lectures was concluded with one given to a BERA seminar on assessment held at Bristol University in July 1991. Patricia Broadfoot, organiser of the seminar, invited me to give my own policy assessment as to the causes lying behind the 1988 Act, and this I attempted to do. Deciding then to collect this particular group of lectures, which tackled the Education 'Reform' Act from a variety of standpoints, I wrote, over the summer of that year (1991) a long essay which set out to link these together, fill in the gaps and so cover the whole field of developments arising from the Act, entitled 'Three Years On'. This, together with some of the lectures already mentioned, and other articles on City Technology Colleges and Grant Maintained Schools was published by Lawrence & Wishart in March 1992 under the title *What Future for Education?* What indeed!

Concentrating again on the two historical books referred to at the start of this chapter, I had hoped that things might now calm down a bit and allow a focus on more long term issues. But this was not to be. Late in the Spring of 1992, following the narrow Conservative victory at the General Election, rumours began to circulate about a new, even more massive Bill than ERA. Although riven by dissension especially on Europe, one issue on which it was hoped unity could be achieved (if under distinctly right wing auspices) was education. It was necessary to take ERA further and 'complete' the reform: indeed (it was now claimed) to lay the legislative basis for the next 25 years. Education, it seemed, had been singled out for further suffering. A White Paper (consultation?) was promised for the Summer, a new Bill would follow.

We had been here before, of course, but now must buckle to again. 'Choice and Diversity' was the title of the White Paper which appeared in July – to general derision, it must be said. A new Secretary of State, John Patten, was said to have written the key chapter but the turgid prose of the document as a whole made little impact. Public discussion of its proposals, however, and our own careful examination, soon revealed a wolf in woolly dress. Lengthy and difficult to grasp, it became apparent that this Bill embodied yet further sharp (even knockout) blows at local authority responsibilities for education, and in particular a number of measures designed to strengthen the crucial opt out clauses of the 1988 Act, and so enhance the rate of that particular transition.

If response to publication of this document was muted there was no strong movement of public opinion against the proposals. It was almost as though the public was punch drunk – or beginning to take a fatalistic attitude in the sense that nothing *could* be done. With its majority in the Commons the government was clearly prepared once more to ride roughshod over such opposition as did express itself to achieve stated goals. There seemed no way to arrest the stampede. A few individuals were prepared to give voice – for instance Tim Brighouse, now a Professor at Keele. Otherwise confusion and a certain despair appeared uppermost.

Then, suddenly, the atmosphere lightened, notably in the educational world. Harassed, rubbished, bullied when possible, at last it mounted a resistance. Indeed this preceded the White Paper by a few days when Eric Bolton, of considerable prestige as former Chief HMI, delivered a measured but scathing attack on prevailing policy at the annual conference of the Council of Local Education Authorities at Liverpool. Under the heading 'Imaginary Gardens with Real Toads', Bolton warned of the dangers inherent in recent policies, sharply criticised a government that listened only to friends in the right-wing coteries referred to, and finished by saying that 'the brave new world' it was creating might be more akin, in reality, 'as Tacitus put it long ago, to the government "making a wilderness and calling it peace"'.

The official response to this widely reported exposure was, as customary, an abusive reaction from Baroness Blatch, but the words continued to resonate. Nor was this all. Through the rest of the summer others added their voices, and again with effect. At the end of August, Paul Black, Professor of Science Education at the Centre for Educational Studies at King's College, London

University, and formerly Chair of the Task Group on Assessment and Testing (TGAT), added his voice in his presidential address to the Education Section of the British Association for the Advancement of Science meeting at Southampton University. Black detailed the debacle over the assessment issue during the period since his original report had been accepted by the then Secretary of State, the now forgotten Kenneth Baker. His address reinforced Bolton's criticism of the 'overwhelming influence' of right-wing pressure groups on government policy, 'notably the Centre for Policy Studies'. As an expert academic researcher who had mistaken the 1988 Act as a force for good and 'given much of his time to trying to help its development', he was 'deeply disappointed and fearful at the outcomes'. Once more Lady Blatch responded with simple abuse.

But now the flood gates were open. Many who mattered had had more than enough. Not that this was a concerted effort – just a determination by a variety of responsible people to have their say. Peter Watkins had already entered the fray, to be joined by Denis Lawton of the London Institute and Duncan Graham, until recently Chief Executive of the National Curriculum Council. In September Caroline Gipps, President of BERA, excoriated Kenneth Clarke for malicious use of supposed research findings about the standard of children's reading to malign the schools – by no means the first use of suspect statistics, nor the last.

What was to be done? Was the new Bill to be driven through without effective opposition? Could the critique courageously made by Eric Bolton, Paul Black and others be more widely and effectively disseminated? To cut a long story short, after discussion with various friends and waiting to see if others would take the initiative as we hoped, Clyde Chitty and I decided that two publications were required and could be prepared. One consisting of the critical addresses just described, the other a short popular exposition and critique of the Education Bill expected in November. Publication of both these could be achieved in February or March 1993.

In the last week or two of October the first of these books, finally titled *Education Answers Back, Critical Responses to Government Policy*, was put together. All the proposed authors whose addresses, articles, etc., we wished to include, among them Bolton and Black, agreed to the proposition as well as all the others we approached (including Fred Jarvis, some of whose hilarious – but also serious – correspondence with the Prime Minister was included). At the very last minute, while checking the proofs early in December, Sir Malcolm Thornton, Tory Chair of the Commons Select Committee on Education, delivered an outstanding address to the De Montfort University in Leicester, very severely critical of government policy. A telephone call gained his immediate agreement for publication in full in the book where it appears as an appendix (too late for the main body of the text), but this greatly added to the authority and impact of the publication as a whole.

Having got this volume together, with Clyde's help, I took off for Harvard University for a few days for a long-planned symposium of the National Academy of Education (of the USA) referred to earlier. On my return at the beginning of November, Clyde and I wrote our critique of the Education Bill, published, as with ERA, in the middle of that month, and, as we expected, differing in no single particular from the proposals originally presented in the White Paper – in this case the 'Consultation' document. This, again, a book of 40,000 words in length, we completed on time, passing the final manuscript to the publishers who, at very short notice, had gallantly agreed to take both books on board, at the beginning of December.

Education Answers Back was launched at a press conference in the Jubilee Room at the House of Commons, reserved for us by Malcolm Thornton, and attended by Frank Judd (recently appointed chief Labour Spokesman in the Lords), Nora David (appointed as his 'second') and others – the Bill was about to move to the Lords for debate and discussion. *SOS Save our Schools* was launched a month later at a convivial informal party at the London Institute of Education. It consisted of a passionate critique of the main thrust of the Bill – the threat to the very existence of local education authorities and the measures included to enhance disruptive market driven forces in educational development.

It was too much to hope that either of these books could do more than strengthen the opposition to the Bill, even though a prolonged defensive action was fought in the Lords involving several very late night (or early morning) sittings. The Bill, or Act as it finally emerged, was by this time certainly something of a shambles, the original script, as the journal *Education* put it (26 March 93), having been 'bruised by the addition of 259 amendments and 18 new clauses with the government alone producing 72 new amendments at the last gasp in the Commons' early in March. Many more were to be introduced, also at the last gasp, in the Lords. 'Lacking vision, consistency and logic, the Education Bill of 1993 is destined to be remembered as an educational folly that sought to find a solution but ended up as part of the problem'.

As the Bill completed its final phases in parliament the government, and particularly John Patten as Secretary of State, was rocked by repeated blows from the teachers' unions relating to their refusal to carry through the testing programme now insisted on. As guests of the newly elected President of the National Union of Teachers (Marian Darke, an old friend) Joan and I were present at the annual conference at Brighton in April 1993 when a unanimous decision to boycott these tests was carried by acclamation. As is well known, this action, supported by other teacher unions, forced a radical re-think of government policy which allayed some of the worst excesses of the testing programme being forced on the schools.

On 26 March 1995 I reached my 80th birthday. Joan was to follow seven months later. As we moved into our ninth decade some relaxation might be thought to be in order – and, indeed, took place. I, personally, now found myself involved in a project I had had in mind for some time, but now brought forward due to developments arising out of presentation of the Seal of the Frankfurt Parliament to Dr. Rita Süssmuth, President of the Bundestag (referred to earlier). This had led to the funding of a research project by a well-known German Trust into the history of the Simon family, involving detailed research into the antecedents, life and activities of my great grand-uncle, Heinrich Simon (1805-60), leading member of the Frankfurt Parliament (and the German revolutionary movement of 1848-49), later an exile in Switzerland; his dramatic death by drowning in the Wallensee, a deep lake near Zürich, had been commemorated by the erection of a monument in his memory at Murg on the lakeside in 1862. The fund for this 'Denkmal' had been raised by local democrats throughout Germany (or, at that time, Prussia). Full-time research on Heinrich now began at the University of Bochum, carried on by Ulrich Hermann, while Detlef Müller, the Professor of Education with whom I had collaborated on an earlier project, decided to focus his own studies on my father, Ernest Darwin Simon. This left the intervening generation, Ernest's father and my grandfather, unattended to. I then decided that the time had come when I should tackle this myself.

Two years fascinating research and study resulted in the publication, early in 1997, of In Search of a Grandfather, Henry Simon of Manchester, 1835-1899. Two university presses turned it down without even asking to see it. I decided to publish it myself (so creating the 'Pendene Press'). Asa Briggs very kindly wrote a fine preface at short notice. As I write, sales have just covered costs. More heart-warming have been the letters received from subscribers, family and others. Indeed more have reacted in this way than to any other of my publications. This has made the project very rewarding.

While I focused on this for two or three years, educational interests were necessarily set aside. But of course this was not altogether possible. For one thing I had found myself tied in again to educational issues when I accepted an invitation from the Council for Educational Advance (CEA) to take on their Presidency. This is an umbrella body which unites trade unions, teacher organisations, educational associations of various kinds, parents and governors in defence of education. Their President had been Richard Hoggart, whom I had known as a lecturer in English at Leicester University during the 1950s, but he wished to resign. The CEA had in fact been set up in 1942 on a resolution moved by my mother within the Workers' Educational

Association, of which she had been a very active vice president.[1] Comprising then the WEA, the Trade Union Congress, the National Union of Teachers (then by far the most important teacher union) and the Co-operative Union, its President for very many years was R.H.Tawney, later succeeded by Hoggart. The CEA had played an important part in whipping up public support for the passage of the 1944 Education Act. This had been its great moment historically. It now led a somewhat tenuous existence, had greatly broadened the number of organisations affiliated, but was not finding it easy to mobilise opinion as in the great days of the 1940s. Partly because of this association (unknown, incidentally, to its 1990 organisers) I was glad to take on the job and give what help I could. The CEA had warmly supported the Forum demonstrative conference against the 1988 Bill, and this disposed me well towards the organisation.

But, in the world of education, much over-excited, essentially political manoeuvring continued, led by macho ministers (Kenneth Clarke, John Patten) who now saw in education a field for political advantage. 'Minister orders Schools to Bring in Streaming' screamed the *Daily Mail* in 1993. 'Patten: Resolute'. No account whatever seemed to be taken of the massive research on this very issue carried through thirty years earlier. It was impossible to stand aside from this new onslaught, and this involved articles in *Forum* and elsewhere – the journal continuing most effectively to monitor the excesses of official policy. This basically, I argued, was an *educational* not a political issue. The education of young children is about empowerment, about the enhancement of initiative, of self-confidence, of creativity. To find the most effective means of promoting these qualities is not easy, 'it is a highly skilled task which makes powerful demands on human ingenuity'. That is the role of the teachers and of all directly concerned with primary education. The attempt of politicians at direct interference and indeed overall control for what are clearly directly political purposes cannot under any circumstances be permitted to succeed. 'That would be to render fruitless the massive humanist endeavour now embodied in our primary schools as well as effectively blighting the future for tens of thousands of children'. It is good to be able to report now, several years later, that the misguided attempts to reintroduce streaming in our primary schools appears as a total failure.

But it was not only primary education that was under threat but also secondary – and indeed the whole concept of comprehensive secondary education. In 1995-96 proponents of the classic, hard-line Burtian school of psychometry once more raised their heads, gaining considerable coverage in the media, and in effect arguing for a return to selective processes of the past. These included the American social scientists Richard Herrnstein and Charles Murray whose *The Bell Curve: intelligence and class structure in American life* (late 1994) led to widespread controversy in the United States, as also here. Taking up the argument, James Tooley now claimed that all children should take an IQ test at the age of 10 years and then be given an 'appropriate' education, just as Burt proposed for his 'ideal community' 45 years ago. And in 1994 Adrian Wooldridge, a strongly right wing (*Daily Mail*) journalist but also Fellow of All Souls College, Oxford, published *Measuring the Mind*, subtitled 'Education and Psychology in England c1860-1990' as mentioned earlier. This combined a history of the mental testing movement with an overt defence of its role in the past and a plea that psychometric techniques be rehabilitated and utilised in educational practice in the future. 'How can raw ability be turned into marketable skills?', the book concludes. 'The psychometrists still have a lot to teach us'.

So I found myself once again drawn back into this field through a Forum article entitled 'IQ Redivivus, or The Return of Selection'. And it now appeared that a radical attempt to impose a selective system in place of comprehensive education was to be expected. Foreshadowed again by a White Paper ('Self-Government for Schools') the Tory government, though apparently tottering on its last legs, determined almost unbelievably on yet one more Education Bill as a means of mobilising electoral support. Selection was to be brought back not only within the whole secondary field but also into primary and even infant schools. A lengthy article in the Spring 1977 issue of

Forum analysed this Bill and its likely effects.

The rest of the story is history. The selective clauses of the Bill were abandoned by the government itself owing to the early promulgation of parliament in preparation for the general election. At that election the government was swept from office, a Labour government taking its place armed with a positive educational programme. The long agony of the past 18 years was over.

EPILOGUE

The solid move towards comprehensive education in England and Wales, approaching the more democratic system of Scotland, meshes directly with global change. All secondary schooling is comprehensive in Scandinavia (Sweden, Norway, Denmark), or essentially non-selective. France has embraced comprehensive education up to the age of 16 and the French are very committed to the system in action. Spain and Portugal provide schools to 16; in Italy the 'Scuola Media' is now the common school for all to the school leaving age, as yet 14. Only Germany and Austria (in Western Europe) retain gymnasia, though not on the narrow model of the English grammar school, thrusting technical provision out of sight. In the Far East Japan, the leading and most successful industrial country, has a complete system of comprehensive education to 15 – indeed in a real sense to 18. This lead has been followed by the 'Tiger' economies of the region, Taiwan and South Korea. In the United States, whatever the shortcomings, the popular system of education has long been comprehensive. There is nothing to apologise for in taking this road, as England, Wales, Scotland have now done; rather there is still a need to catch up with the rest of the world.

Up to the age of 16 all children should have the opportunity to experience a full, all-round education embodying the humanities, arts, sciences and technology – this is and always has been the aim of comprehensive education. In such schools there are no blind alleys, no once-and-for-all tests to cut off or divest children from access to learning. Opportunities remain open for all.

Well-equipped schools of this type serve their own neighbour-hood in every locality. Such is the objective. To achieve this schools not only need generous resources in terms of buildings, equipment and staff; they also need to evolve the relevant peda-gogical means carefully honed to ensure that all children are effectively assisted in their learning. This is an area where much has been lacking, in both primary and secondary schools.

My own life in education, covering sixty years of active involvement, has passed through different phases, but central, in the latter stages especially, has been attainment for all children in this country of a full primary and secondary education, as outlined above. Historical study over these years has shown that periods of advance in the past have too often been followed by powerful and deliberate moves to turn back the clock – or to direct breakthroughs into innocuous channels. This is true of the great surge forward in the 1890s decimated by legislative and administrative means early this century; of the hopes and plans arising from new circumstances in both world wars, each time doused and extinguished by succeeding governments.

The slow emergence of a consensus on educational advance in the mid-1990s, which found concrete expression in the general election of 1 May 1997 creates a new situation. Here, then, is a programme for the 21st century for any government worth its salt. The need now is to go even further, and finally create a genuinely national system of education. Current provisions, historically based, are no longer acceptable. Such must be the agenda for the future.

NOTES

1. According to a note in my parents' cutting book kept by my father, the result of the vote for the Vice Presidency of the WEA in 1956 read as follows:

    (i)   Lady Simon, 281 votes
    (ii) Hugh Gaitskell, 263 votes
    (iii) R.A. Butler, 164 votes

NAME INDEX

Delamont, Sara, 133
Dent, Harold, 45, 74, 85
Dobrée, Bonamy, 34
Donnison, David, 106
Drake, Barbara, 30-2
Dunn, Bob, 165

Eaglesham, Eric, 110
Eccles, J.R., 8
Ede, J. Chuter, 29, 31
Eden, Anthony, 25
Edgeworth, Richard Lovell, 72
Eggleston, Jim F., 132
Eggleston, John, 100
Eliot, T.S., 60
Elkonin, D.B., 97
Elvin, Lionel, 31, 103, 111
Eysenck, H.J., 119, 122

Finney, Albert, 55
Fisher, R.S., 11
Fleshner, E.A., 97
Florence, Sargant, 35
Ford, Boris, 12
Fox, Charles, 7
Fraser, Hugh, 46
Freeland, George, 87, 90-3
Frow, Ruth and Edmund, 152
Fry, Margery, 34
Fryer, Bob, 152-3
Fujioka, Professor, 148

Gale, Margot (see Kettle), 33, 43
Galperin, P. Ya., 81
Galton, Maurice, 132ff, 142-3, 146
Garrett, John, 76
Gentile, 18
Gipps, Caroline, 169
Godwin, William, 124
Goerdeler, Carl, 25
Gramsci, Antonio, 18
Gray, John, 71
Green, Cecil and Ida, 147
Green, T.H., 154
Greenwood, Anthony, 29
Greenwood, Arthur, 29
Gurrey, P., 18, 21-3

Hahn, Kurt, 8-9
Halifax, Lord, 25, 42
Hamilton, David, 132, 161
Hamley, Professor, 19
Hancock, David, 165

Heath, Edward, 117
Heim, Alice, 77
Hemming, James, 76
Herbart, J.F., 48
Herman, Ulrich, 172
Hill, Christopher, 35
Hirst, Paul, 110, 145
Himmelweit, Hilde, 133
Hodgkin, Thomas, 71
Hoggart, Richard, 172-3
Honey, John, 149
Hopkinson, General, 46
Horio, Teruhisa, 148-9
Horner, Francis, 73
Horsbrugh, Florence, 68
Hoskins, W.G., 112
Husen, Thorsten, 148

Isaacs, Susan, 20

Jackson, Brian, 94, 95, 103
James, Eric, 85
Jasman, Anne, 135-6
Jeffreys, M.V.C., 17
Jensen, Arthur, 118-9, 122
Jones, Jack, 152
Jones, Morgan, 29, 31
Joseph, Keith, 158-9
Judd, Frank, 170
Judges, A.V., 74

Kerr, Jack, 100, 114
Kettle, Arnold, 33
Kettle, Margot (see Gale), 33
King, Raymond, 88, 96, 106
Klugmann, James, 10, 33, 37, 70-1
Knight, Christopher, 107
Knights, L.C., 34
Kogan, Maurice, 93, 156
Koo, Wellington, 37
Krutetski, V.A., 97

Lauwerys, Joseph, 17-8
Lawson, John, 110
Lawton, Denis, 169
Leavis, F.R., 23
Lee, Jennie, 87
Leontiev, A.N., 81, 97
Lester Smith, W.O., 156
Levin, Deana, 80
Lindsay, A.D., 41
Linfield, Eric, 91, 93
Lofthouse, Charles, 19

SUBJECT INDEX